Catholic Alcoholic

Catholic Alcoholic

A Witness to
Addiction and
Redemption

ANNETTA SANOW SUTTON

BEAVER'S POND
PRESS

The excerpts from Alcoholics Anonymous is reprinted with permission of Alcoholics Anonymous World Services, Inc. "(AAWS"). Permission to reprint the excerpt does not mean that AAWS has reviewed or approved the contents of this publication, or that AAWS necessarily agrees with the views expressed herein. A.A. is a program of recovery from alcoholism which are patterned after A. A., but which address other problems, or in any other no A.A. context, does not imply other wise. Additionally, while A.A. is a spiritual program, A.A. is not a religious program. Thus, A.A. is not affiliated or allied with any sect, denomination, or specific religious belief.

ISBN: 978-1-59298-471-8
Library of Congress Control Number: 2012905644

Cover design by David Spohn
Interior design by Ryan Scheife, Mayfly Design
Typeset in Whitman

Printed in the United States of America
First Printing: 2012

16   15   14   13   12   5   4   3   2   1

Beaver's Pond Press, Inc.
7108 Ohms Lane
Edina, MN 55439-2129
(952) 829-8818
www.BeaversPondPress.com

To order, visit www.BeaversPondBooks.com
or call (800) 901-3480. Reseller discounts available.

For my children: Amy, Emy, Jenny, Chet, and Bret

Acknowledgments

It takes a village to write a book. My gratitude is without limits.

Thank you to:

My early editors, Nicole Sutton and Laurel Johnson, for your tireless encouragement and my editor Jennifer Manion, I am forever grateful.

Amy Quale and Ryan Scheife, a credit to the next generation, and Beaver's Pont Press and its visionaries.

My friend, Clara Helvig, who continuously encouraged me to write "my book."

Kathleen Norris and Mary Morris for showing me how. And to the Loft Literary Center for providing the place.

The Benedictines and all the religious who formed and provided a model of faith. To the pastoral priests and bishops who showed me how to love and believe in the faith of my ancestors.

The Sanow family, especially Laurel, for showing me my roots. Don Sanow who showed me over my entire life how the Sanows loved. John Sanow, my nephew, who provided support and love at an extremely important juncture.

Elizabeth Pearl, John Lemke, and Helen Ferder who provided me the Braun history.

Damian McElrath for mentoring me not only through this project but also at a significant difficult stage encouraging me to "keep going and continuing to do the good work God has called you to do." You, Damian, are a sign of God's continued love.

The two magnificent bishops I worked with who taught me the best in ministry.

Patrick and Mary for providing the truth.

Anthony who provided love.

Precious Aunt Mildred Young for loving me and loving your brother and my father.

Uncle Guy and Aunt Lil Graham for coming through for my family more than once.

My Braun cousins for sharing your parents, my beloved aunts and uncles, and for our laughter.

My Saint Martin's sisters for constant faithful friendship.

Mariah Elizabeth thank you for teaching what is important and to "Dream, Dream, Dream."

And to Cece and Mary, thank you for letting me love you.

Introduction

"I love you."

Tears ran along the bridge of my nose. In front of me, six granite stones (LaVone, Karren, Wally, Harry, Joe, and LaVerna) and behind them, resting in the prairie grasses, four more (Elizabeth "Bessie," Ferdinand, Ferdie, and Lawrence).

Green Hill Cemetery. Lemmon, South Dakota.

A stone. A story. A reflection.

My tears drip from my chin.

I am a Catholic. I am not an alcoholic. I do, however, love alcoholics. All of them. The disease, and the people living with and in it, consumes every aspect of my life, as does the Catholic Church. The Roman Catholic Church. From the moment of birth, it has surrounded my life. Incense has bled from my veins. Organ music has filled my ears. Holy water has dripped from my head.

The church was the center of our family, the center of my existence. Catholic traditions, liturgical cycles, the seven sacraments, Holy Week, holy days, Advent, Christmas, Lent, rogation days, and the rosary all supplied our life with direction and structure. I loved the bricks, mortar, and statues, especially the rare ones with smiles. In our parish, gentle Saint Joseph had a smile. As a child, I loved him. In adulthood, I understood why. He became a father figure. I wanted a man in my life like Saint Joseph. Someone gentle.

Catholics experience the mystery and the messiness almost immediately. Shortly after birth is baptism. Then guilt, which comes early and stays late.

The disease of alcoholism thrives in it. On it.

Alcoholism and Catholicism: both are paradoxes. They capture life and death. Joy and suffering. Faith and doubt. Compassion and abuse. Death and resurrection.

They are paradoxes, but parallels. Catholic. Alcoholic.

Writing this book, I gathered reflections from many memories and sources. Research included Ellis Island; Westchester County, New York; Cherokee County, Iowa; Pretty Rock, North Dakota; Green Hill Cemetery. Interviews. Life stories.

But my story's roots come from a deeper source: my mother's journal.

"My God," I said kept saying. Astonished, I could not put it down.

Her daughter was writing her own journal.

My face hurt. I felt blood in my mouth; it seeped through my lips. Standing in our newly completed dream home, I held our infant son close, tears streaming down my face.

"I am going to kill you," he slurred as he threw the bottle of catsup.

I ducked. It barely missed my head. The catsup splattered as it hit the freshly painted wall.

"Blow your head off," he ranted as he fell toward the oak kitchen table. "Don't you think I know who you are?" he sneered. "You are a woman with a dead father and two dead sisters."

I tasted salt as my tears ran into my mouth. With the tears, fear, coupled with numbness. I thought, "What happened to my high school sweetheart?

The alcoholic rage had become common. This was not his first. It was just another Saturday night in our home.

Scheduled to play the organ for Sunday Mass, I thought in a panic, "How will I look in the morning? We can't miss Mass. Do I have enough makeup to cover my face? Will the bruises show through?"

Why did I stay? The babies? Fear? Finances? Love? My own mother's retort? I had many reasons. But they weren't real answers. Not yet.

My other three children—the beautiful blond girls we had had together—were asleep. And close by those three sleeping beauties were the dresses I had laid out for Sunday Mass.

"Buck up." I told myself. "No one needs to know." I kept smiling.

Sunday morning, I dressed our four stunningly beautiful children, the girls in their matching dresses and our baby in the cuddly blue suit. The five of us walked to Saint Bonaventure, the church of my childhood. Father Francis, the military veteran turned priest, smiled as we entered. I smiled and greeted him. My lip stung. He did not notice.

I stepped up to the organ, turned on the switch, organized the four children by handing the baby to Amy, eight years old, the oldest. The children sat still. "Make me a channel of your peace," sang the congregation as my fingers softly played the white keys.

No one knew of the cover-up, common in an alcoholic home. The makeup worked.

~

Jack refused to follow the treatment center's recommendations. "I am not going to follow that shit." There'd be no recovery for him. And no amount of pleas or tears would change his mind.

Then two words fell from my lips. "Enough. Leave."

He did.

Today, he sits in a chair with wheels.

~

"I am made in the image and likeness of God." Only when I stopped allowing the vessel to be destroyed did I begin to feel alive again. Pain brought awareness. Depth. Compassion. The little house on the prairie provided the groundwork. A church provided the foundation. And twelve steps provided me with a way to fully appreciate both the little house and the church.

~

A few years later, I picked up the phone in my office as the Roman Catholic diocesan director of the office of separated, divorced, and widowed to hear familiar words: "My husband's drunk." The sobbing woman's voice was distraught.

"He spends money we don't have. Hits me. He has been with other women. I cannot take it anymore. Please, will you talk to him?"

Assuring her of help, encouraging her to breathe, I inquired about her safety. Continuing unabated, she said, "He will listen to you. He respects you. Will you talk to him? Please?" In nineteen years of working in the church, I had routinely heard such pleas. They were common. They were pleas that were folded in with poverty, infidelity, racism, sexism, and physical, emotional, and sexual abuse, often including rape.

Ethically, I was prohibited from calling her husband. Surprisingly, he called me. The call began with the usual litany of placing blame on the other. In this incidence, the problem was his wife. In the midst of his complaining, he abruptly stopped and stated, "She thinks I am an alcoholic, Annetta. Do you?"

Intervention, I had learned years before, is never about a professional answering a question like this. It is about asking the question. I asked the woman's husband, "Has alcohol caused problems in your life physically? Socially?" No answer. Continuing, I added my own litany, asking "Has your drinking impacted you in your familial relationships, emotionally, legally, financially, or spiritually? If the response is yes," I suggested, "and if you are not an alcoholic now, the probability is that you are well on your way."

The response on the other end of the phone was emphatic, angry. "I can't be alcoholic. I am Catholic."

I smiled. Listening to his angry response, I scribbled words on the notepad in front of me: "Catholic," and below it, "Alcoholic." Then I stared at what I suddenly saw. The words contained the same letters, with one exception, the *t*.

The cross. My response to his statement was two words—in some sense, the same word with the one odd letter, the *t*.

Edith Stein (1891–1942), philosopher, Jew, atheist, convert to Catholicism, Carmelite nun, and martyr, spoke of the science of the cross. Paradox. Death and resurrection. Life and death. Returning from death to life. Finding Christ in the cross. Finding faith in suffering. Joy in the resurrection. Choosing construction rather than destruction.

Catholicism and alcoholism go together like the sacramental commingling of water and wine during Mass. For many baptized Catholics, Catholicism and alcoholism become one. Therein lies how a disease and a church impact millions of lives, mine included. Therein lies a story that might be told about any church, any belief system, or any nonbeliever.

For me, through infant baptism, Catholicism and alcoholism became imbedded in me just as my DNA was embedded in me. It was—is—a church filled with saints and sinners. Compassion and abuse. Together, the disease and the church affect the mind, body, and spirit. The disease of alcoholism takes the sufferer, and those who love him or her, through a living hell. When those who are affected by the disease seek recovery, a new life opens.

Christ said to Peter the apostle, "Upon this rock, I will build my church." That church, filled with fallible beings, can be a place of searching, a place that offers an experience of faith to those who seek and search. It is a church rich in solace, tradition, fallibility, reality, community, and pain.

In my case, a disease and a faith, both of which I knew little of when I was first carried to the door of the church, took me to the depths of questioning—and then to peace.

When you live the sacramental life of the church, you taste the suffering of others. You also live it. Yet in this church, as in other churches, synagogues, mosques, and in society in general, when it comes to the suffering brought on by the disease of alcoholism, one often feels judgment, criticism, loneliness, and isolation instead of compassion and communion.

Add to this isolation Catholic guilt, which, as I said, begins early and stays late. We Catholics attempt to assuage the guilt in the confessional. For most, it works. For those suffering from the debilitating disease of addiction, the shame can be so great that the alcoholic often does not believe or feel God's grace, despite its plenteousness. But when recovery occurs, poor Catholics often become better Catholics.

In my thirty-five years of working in parishes—nineteen of them as a diocesan director in the Roman Catholic Church—and today in my work in the spiritual care department at Hazelden, the distinguished addiction treatment center, or in my work volunteering in downtown Minneapolis homeless shelters, or in my own home, the pleas for help have never stopped.

Chapter One

"It's a girl," Doctor MacDonald said as he pulled me from a grieving womb. My mother birthed me in McKennan Hospital, which was run by the Presentation Sisters and was located twenty miles east of our home in Sioux Falls, South Dakota, with the help of the Irish doctor, Mom and Dad's friend. The hospital bill for the ten-day stay was $99. The name on the birth certificate read AnEtta Marie Sanow. However, in my baby book, Mom spelled my name Annetta, beginning my life-long confusion about my name, my identity.

I was born to an Irish-German mother and German father who had recently settled in a small, Irish hamlet: Montrose, South Dakota. It was a Midwest town filled with homespun Irish warmth and hospitality, set among rolling, verdant, lush farm fields. The small town's streets were lined with manicured lawns, colorful flower gardens, and clean, well-cared-for homes. Front porches were common fare. In the evenings and on weekends, people strolled from one home to another, visiting.

From the west, a hill brought passersby to Main Street. There, on Saturday nights, a gazebo provided a place for local talent to present weekly community concerts. When I was a small child, Mom dressed us kids in our finest for those Saturday night concerts. The smell of popcorn would waft through the air, beginning my lifelong love of popcorn. It was pure magic.

Our home, purchased the year of my birth, was a clapboard sided home with burgundy-flowered-linoleum, a refuge. A small creek meandered through its backyard; in the spring, the creek sometimes overflowed its banks, flooding the yard, the air filled with the sweet smell of apple blossoms that graced the trees in our orchard. Those delicate blossoms were followed in the summer and early fall by deliciously tart apples. Mom made pies, applesauce, and succulent jellies and jams.

Two people carried me from McKennan Hospital home to Montrose: my mother and father. Just a few days later, as is Catholic tradition, another two, with my parents, carried me the scant blocks from our home to Saint Patrick's Church, a lovely brick Romanesque structure, for my baptism. These were William and Elaine Sanow, my godparents, at that time the only other Catholics in Dad's family.

My mother. LaVerna Katherine Braun. A fascinating woman, from the rich soil of the Dakotas.

My dad. Alfred Johannes Wilhelm Sanow, called A. J. or Al Sanow. World War I veteran. Twenty-five years older than Mom. Born in Cherokee County, Iowa.

Al Sanow adored his wife, and she, him. It is written in their love letters. The people surrounding them witnessed it. They danced to the *Tennessee Waltz*, and he sang to her, *Mocking Bird Hill*. Told often of their parents' gentle, passionate love, we children basked in the knowledge. "Ohhhh," Dad's older sister, Amelia, whom we called Aunt Mellie, told me, her voice trailing off as she remembered. "Your dad loved your mother, and she loved him. The only argument

I knew your parents had was over your father driving thirty miles back to Sioux Falls to buy the little dishes he promised Karren." Karren: my older sister, their first daughter. Aunt Mellie continued, "Your mom was furious, said to your dad, 'Al, there is no sense to driving all that way for some dishes we can buy later.' Your father said, 'A promise is a promise. And I will never break a promise to my children.'" For the round-trip, Dad drove sixty miles in the old 1949 blue Chevy and kept the promise to his two-year-old daughter.

I learned the backstory of these two pivotal adults in my life much later. As a very young girl in Montrose, I only knew Dad was a doter. He doted on Mom and my older siblings, Wally and Karren. Then me.

There had been another baby, the cause of Mom's grieving womb: a boy, Russell August, conceived shortly after Karren's birth. He lived only a few days. I followed Russell. My conception and birth was impacted by Russell's death. His life had mattered, especially to Mom, and ultimately to me, the one born after. Fourteen months after I arrived, LaVone was born. We called her Vonnie. Satisfied with their family, LaVerna and Al were happy, blissful.

Prior to having children and when she and Dad lived in Canistota, a short drive from Montrose, Mom had been one of South Dakota's first female business owners. She and Dad even bought a building. "Let's have a name-the-shop contest," she had said to Dad one day. He agreed, and they solicited entries. The beauty shop was named LaSan, and the winner received a free shampoo, cut, and style.

Naturally gregarious and with real business acumen, Mom provided hair care for community members, both living and dead. In her shop, she styled the coifs of the living. Working beside the local mortician, Archie Odell, she fixed the hair of the deceased.

When she and Dad moved the family to Montrose just before I was born, she relocated the beauty shop to our house, giving Mom ample time to tend to business and her growing flock.

"You were the best baby." It was one of the few things Mom told me about my childhood. "You just played in the playpen while I worked. Never demanded anything." A note Mom wrote in my baby book was apologetic—"I did not have enough time for you"—referring to Vonnie's birth not long after mine.

Dad worked as a field representative for South Dakota Benevevolent Society. Ours was an idyllic life. Surrounded by love.

Life changed on April 13, 1952.

"Honey, you go. Enjoy coffee with your friends," Dad often suggested to Mom before he left for work. That early spring morning was no different. It began with Dad making breakfast. Karren and Wally, already in school a few blocks from our home. Dad said, "The two little ones will stay with me." Ever the doting husband and father, Dad wanted his wife to have a minute to herself. Tending his two youngest, my sister Vonnie, not yet a year old, and me, past two, Dad went to brush his teeth.

People question when memory begins. For me, it was just past two. Dad's last day on earth. No one was there to tell me what happened in the bathroom on April 13, 1952. I know for myself. It is a vivid memory.

My short legs hang over the bathtub, feet dangling. I'm watching the man who gave me life brush his teeth. Vonnie chirps in the empty but safe bathtub behind me. Dad turns from the sink, picks up Vonnie. I follow him as he carries

Vonnie to the living room and then lies down on the sofa. Vonnie and I crawl on his chest. His eyes are closed.

I remember people entering; they carry my father out of our home. They take him to the hospital.

I did not understand what was happening. I could not understand.

My father died a few hours later. A perfectly healthy, slender, fifty-two-year-old man. Dead. Heart disease. I was a child. I did not understand.

"You are built like your dad. You look like your dad," people said. "And you're the spitting image of Aunt Mellie and your Grandma Sanow." I loved it when people said things like this. It connected me. Later came the repercussions.

Mostly I was told little about Dad. Snippets. I was told Dad hated alcohol. So did Mom. Why? Understanding, too, comes in increments.

At the moment of my father's death, the relationship between my mother and I was sealed. I lost both parents that day. Years later, I intellectually understood the term "lost child," but at the time, I lived it. I was lost. I remember feeling absence, abandonment. It clung to my often-wet pillow at night, when I missed Dad especially. This feeling later sent me on a decade's long, lonely journey to find him. Yet later, it urged me to acknowledge the longing I felt to figure out how to live with what I had lost.

"Cute as buttons" my cousin Lynn described my sister Vonnie and me at the time of Dad's death. She told me years later that she had attended Dad's funeral with Mom's brother, Carl. She remembered that Vonnie and I played as the adults mourned. What else would we have done? We were children. Babies.

Irish Catholic tradition was to hold a wake over the body

in the home, prior to the funeral; it provided a time for the soul to take leave. Death, according to Irish custom, does not occur abruptly. The wake also provides families and friends with time to pray, grieve, and celebrate the deceased.

So Mom brought Dad back to the warmth of our home, to be surrounded by the woman and children he loved. Family and friends came to love us. He lay in our dining room. I remember the box in the house. I do not remember Dad being in it. There was quiet talking. Crying. Food.

Mom never recovered from his death. Neither did his four children. After the wake and then Dad's funeral, Mom did not talk about it. The pain was too raw.

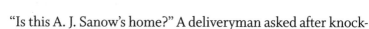

"Is this A. J. Sanow's home?" A deliveryman asked after knocking on our door a few weeks after Dad's death.

"Yes," Mom replied.

The man continued, "I am here to deliver the piano." Mother assured the man he had the wrong home. "This piano," the man stated, "was bought on this day." He pointed to a date. "Paid for and signed by this man." He pointed to a signature. "With the instruction for it to be delivered on this day." He pointed to a second date.

Mom looked at the signature. It was Dad's. Two days before he died, he had bought and paid for a new piano. Even in death, he surprised her. He wanted to give his children the opportunity to learn on a beautiful instrument. We did.

Montrose, South Dakota, was a haven for a young widow who, by an early age, had already buried her parents, a brother, a child, and now her first love and husband. She was twenty-seven; a single mother of four young children.

Chapter Two

Laverna Katherine Braun Sanow, and later, Kittelson.

She was our Rose Kennedy.

Mom kept a journal. It's a page-turner, her backstory, intense. All grit and determination. The journal's simple descriptions belie her parents' difficult, early lives together. Ferd and Bessie. They tamed the plains like the other sturdy immigrants. It became their jobs, their lives. The callous, unbending harshness of the land also took many an immigrant's life.

Mom came by her strength naturally. Good stock. Ireland and Germany folded together in a woman with a strong Catholic faith. "More Catholic than the Pope." It was a common expression people used to describe Mom.

Ancestral homes breed traditions, whet our faith. Ancestral homes also often incubate the disease of alcoholism. Genetic predisposition. Mom brought both to the lives of her children.

LaVerna was an enigma, a feminist when feminism was not in vogue. Showing her to be a pioneer in many things, Mom's journal reads like a Laura Ingalls Wilder book, but without the romanticism. The story it tells details one half of my foundation. It outlines that juncture where Catholicism and alcoholism crossed in my personal history. That crossroads was destined by family bonds, perseverance, faith and abuse.

In the journal are the words: "She's dead. Your mother is dead." Mom's father, Ferd, said to them as he fell into a chair, bereft, after returning from the hospital. Pregnant for the seventh time, his wife had succumbed to peritonitis after giving birth, and the baby had died, too. Elizabeth "Bessie" Tracy Braun had been in her early forties. Mom was just an adolescent girl.

It was the first of multiple tragedies. A second followed quickly. A horrible accident that left mom and her siblings alone.

Mom's journal continues. "Three months after Mom died, we heard Doc Totten say to Dad, 'Ferd, I will take away the pain.'" Doc Totten, the sole local physician, miracle worker, and Ferd's friend, was trying to save his life. (Years later, Doc Totten's granddaughter Kathleen Norris and I became friends, our South Dakota prairie roots forged by the two men.)

The only miracle Doc Totten could perform that day was to administer morphine. Ferd's legs were gone. Blown away. A train had hit him during a catastrophic fire at the railroad yards in Lemmon, South Dakota. Doc Totten couldn't save Ferd's legs and couldn't save him.

Mom was fifteen. She was orphaned along with five brothers: Lawrence, nineteen; Carl, seventeen; James, twelve; Ferdinand, eight; and Wally, six. In a world cruel to them, the six young Braun siblings developed survival techniques that served them the rest of their lives.

Mom loved her brothers first and foremost. It was an intense and strong bond. We all knew it. The bond between the six Braun siblings remained until death. Even their spouses knew not to intrude upon the sibling bond.

Mom was born LaVerna Katherine Braun on May 22, 1919, to "Ferd" Ferdinand Braun and "Bessie" Elizabeth Tracy Braun. She began her life on the prairies of Dakota. Pretty Rock, North Dakota. It was a place, not a town. From those humble beginnings, Mom grew into a stunningly beautiful young woman.

Bessie's parents, my great-grandparents, Anna Elizabeth Bennett and James Patrick Tracy, had emigrated from Dublin, Ireland, disowned due to what then was considered a mixed marriage. Anna was English, Protestant, and a domestic. James's family, the Tracys, had been wealthy Irish Catholic landowners. The Tracy family looked down upon such a relationship. Mom called the repercussions of their relationship and their leaving the Irish homeland the "Tracy Curse." Given the genealogy and history, early tragic deaths, rages of alcoholism, and Catholic guilt. She may have been on to something, as the Irish say.

I loved listening to the stories Mom and her brothers told about their parents, my grandparents. The stories were rich in history, although sullied by tragedy, and echoed with Irish humor. They were flavored with intense laughter. The laughter kept the foundation alive.

"They were strong people." That's what Mom said about my grandparents. Bessie and Ferd Braun were married in 1912 at Saints Peter and Paul Catholic Church outside Hebron, North Dakota. Mom's eyes filled with tears when she shared their wedding picture with me.

Years later, I worked in the same dioceses that housed Saints Peter and Paul Catholic Church. The building was still standing, alone, uninhabited, abandoned yet determined on the North Dakota plains, encircled by golden wheat fields. Strong, like my grandparents. Stoic German immigrants had built it.

Ferd's father, Joseph Braun, my great-grandfather, lies buried in the cemetery beside the church. He helped build this testimony to a raw, deep, and indestructible faith. The building was constructed with local fieldstone held together with a kind of mortar called gumbo. Gumbo, a blend of clay and sand, mixed with straw and water they had to haul from a distant lake by wagons. Today, the mortar still holds the stone together.

I once asked, "How do you think Grandma and Grandpa Braun met?" The reply: "Probably on the section line." The section line determined the homesteaders' boundaries or areas of land. I suspect they met at a basket social, a ritual in which a young man would buy and then often court the young woman who made the goodies and assembled the basket. Basket socials were common in their day. Or perhaps they met at a barn dance. Or at church.

∼

"The Tracys and Brauns lived immigrants' lives on the newly homesteaded plains of North Dakota," Mom wrote. After emigrating from Ireland, the Tracys bore seven children. Grandma Bessie was one of three girls and four boys. The

Brauns had emigrated from Germany via Russia, and gave life to thirteen children on the prairies of Dakota near Hebron, North Dakota; Grandpa Ferd was third oldest. They had been greeted by Lady Liberty on their way to Ellis Island. Ambrose, the youngest of the thirteen, was born on the ship coming to America.

The Brauns were of stoic, hardworking, unemotional German stock. The Tracys were an emotional, strong, and loving people. The integration of the two strong Catholic families came to fruition in Mom.

"My God," I said, and kept saying, astonished, as I read the journal. I could not put it down.

After their wedding, Ferd and Bessie moved to what is now Corson County, South Dakota, and into their first home, a house made of stone. They became mail carriers. For three years, they delivered mail by horse and buggy. During that time, babies began and kept coming, with Carl following Lawrence, the first of six.

One night, the stone house was struck by lighting as the young family slept. Fire raged throughout the house. Ferd attempted to smother the fire, to save their meager belongs. In the melee, Ferd, standing six feet four inches, suffered burns on his hips, thighs, and legs. Bessie ran from the flames with the little boys. Their lives were saved, but their paltry belongings were lost.

It was not the only time that the horror of fire haunted the Brauns. Fire seemed to follow Ferd. Forced to move, the family found a piece of land on the Grand River. The bruised-but-not-beaten family moved into a small log cabin on the Grand River with a few staples, their only mode of transportation, a horse-driven wagon, a cow tied behind.

Eventually with the help of Bessie's brother, the Braun's built a small clapboard house. It was stark and lonely, set against the ocean blue sky that turned a magnificent pink as the earth moved on its axes in early morning and gold and red in the evening. Empty land stretched far as the eye could see. No neighbors, no friends, not a car. It was twenty-five miles to a store.

With two small children, the young bride worked beside her young groom. Horses yoked, Ferd attempted to break the brutal, inflexible land to plant the sacred, scarce seeds of wheat and oats. They raised sheep, hogs, and chickens. Kerosene lamps provided light at night, while a wood stove supplied heat and a place for Bessie to cook the meals that fed their growing family. It also heated the flat iron she used to press their homemade clothing for Mass miles away at Saint Mary's Catholic Church in Lemmon, South Dakota.

When the brutal Dakota prairie winters became unbearable, Ferd, with a horse and wagon, secured coal from a coal mine miles from their home. They used it to heat the small house and to cook. It protected the family.

There was no bathroom, no running water. The toilet was a little house built over a hole. Old catalogs provided toilet tissue.

Bessie became pregnant with my mom. In her isolation and loneliness, Bessie wanted to be with her mother when the baby was born. She longed to see her family. Ferd loaded the boys and his very pregnant wife in the buggy, and he set out, like Joseph with Mary, to fight the forty miles of dirt roads to the Tracy ranch.

The roads were miserable and sloppy from the spring rains. They arrived at Pretty Rock in time for the birth of LaVerna Katherine, my mother. Returning to their homestead, they continued to eke out a living on the sparse, unyielding land. Following the birth of their only daughter, Bessie birthed three more boys on the barren prairie. First there was James, then Ferdinand, whom they nicknamed Ferdie, and then the youngest, Wally.

Eventually, more people took up claims on the land, becoming neighbors. Bessie wrote to her sisters, "Neighbors, a most welcomed addition of women to visit, who, too, find the unforgiving prairie a place of isolation."

Bessie and Ferd felt strongly about education. So Ferd, along with the neighborhood men, built a country school a little over a mile from the Braun place. The Tracy women were natural-born teachers. Bessie was self-taught, but her sister Marie was a teacher who taught in a one-room school close to their home at Pretty Rock. On Ferd's side, Grandpa Joseph Braun served on one of the first school boards in North Dakota.

Since the school was a distance for little legs to cover, Bessie securely tied her young children on the family horse, sending her treasures to school on the loyal stead. The teacher untied the blessed bundle of children upon arrival. Beside the one-room schoolhouse stood a little barn that

Ferd and a neighbor man had filled with hay. There, the students' horses ate silently, waiting to return their sacred cargo home.

———

"'We'll milk the cows," we'd call back to Mom as we ran to the barn," my mother wrote in her journal. Prior to leaving for school each morning, the six children milked the cows, every child provided with a special animal. Each had named his or her cow—the relationship was intimate.

After collecting the milk in galvanized buckets, the children carried the milk to their mother, who separated the white gold using an apparatus called a separator. She'd then pour the cream and whole milk cautiously onto the homegrown, homemade oatmeal. The leftover milk, called skimmed milk, went to the calves or pigs.

Saturday was butter-churning day. The wooden churn stood waiting passively until Bessie poured the cream into its top. The children then turned the side handle until its contents became butter. Bessie used carrot juice, pressed from the summer carrot crop and reserved in the root cellar, to color the luscious butter yellow. The fresh, delectable buttermilk provided a treat for small taste buds and made succulent pancakes, which Bessie topped with the fresh butter and choke cherry syrup. Life was good.

The words in Mom's journal nearly jump off the page. "The Grand River ambled through the land close to our house, bringing a cool, refreshing place to ward off the heat as we six blondes swam and played in the summer. The frozen Grand gave way to a winter wonderland, a virtual haven to skate, sled, and coast with whatever we and our neighborhood friends could amuse ourselves." Mom concluded, "We made our own fun."

Butchering was done in the fall. Mom tells of Ferd killing a cow, two pigs, and two sheep for their winter store. Bessie, with her young helpmates, canned. Golden peaches and bright yellow pears, bought by the crate, filled Mason and Ball jars, which then sat tall and proud beside canned chicken and vegetables. After a day of canning, Bessie delighted when pinging sounds broke the night silence, indicating that the jars were well sealed.

The root cellar, a place dug out for preserving the summer and fall harvests and to store the winter food, filled to the brim each fall. Among the cellar's treasures were jams and jellies made by Bessie from wild berries, tenderly picked by small hands. The precious preserves were luscious spread on Bessie's freshly made bread. The root cellar also provided a place of safety when storms, especially tornadoes, threatened.

Baptized at Saint Mary's Catholic Church in Lemmon, South Dakota, the six Braun children at one point attended school at Saint Mary's Grade School until it closed, later reopening. This sacrifice was significant for a family striving to survive and living twenty-five miles away; they accessed Lemmon most likely only by horse and buggy. Bessie and Ferd, raised in strong Catholic families, felt the sacrifice was important. They had instilled in the children an early devotion to the Blessed Mother, and they valued Catholic education knowing it wasn't better than the little prairie school, it was different, so they sent their children, despite the difficulty.

It was at Saint Mary's where the family came under the influence of Sister Marsha and Father Falkins. "Mom and Dad wanted us to attend Catholic school and we did for a time," Mom wrote. "Dad delivered us to the dormitory and we stayed the week until Dad returned Friday to take us home."

Later, when Mom shared the story, I was never clear how long this went on. Mom was in the fifth grade when the school closed. But it was obviously meaningful to her, and I believe this experience was behind her encouragement and efforts to make her own children comfortable when most of us attended private Catholic boarding high school.

When the weather cooperated, the pioneer Braun family thought that they could turn their dream of a successful farm into a real possibility. But drought more often dashed the dreams. And when it hit, they barely survived. Hunger beckoned. Bessie wrote to her sister of the long hours, difficult work, and constant loneliness. The cows dried up. Chickens stopped laying. Drought surrounded them.

But they kept trying. Taming the plains was brutal. In a photograph from this time, Mom stands with her brothers, beautiful Bessie beside them, all in tattered clothes. The hard prairie life is etched on Bessie's face. It shows her exhaustion. Her hair is limp against her neck.

The family sold the farm in 1930. The Brauns moved into town—Lemmon, South Dakota—and bought a cafe. The Great Depression was beginning; the bottom fell out for everyone. In just two years, Ferd sold the cafe in Lemmon and bought a cafe in McLaughlin, South Dakota. No one in the country had money to spend, so he sold the McLaughlin café and the family returned to Lemmon filled with fear of impending doom.

The disaster realized. In 1935, shortly after the move back to Lemmon, Bessie died in her early forties, contracting peritonitis after the stillbirth of her seventh child. The same infection would cause the death of her namesake granddaughter, Karren Elizabeth, thirty-five years later.

Ferd and her children were devastated. Bessie's death influenced her six children and everything they did for the rest of their lives. A motherless home is a home without heart. A father can provide love and security, but the heart of a home rests in the body of a mother who carried her children under her heart.

Without Bessie, Ferd found a companion, a mistress, a lover, and a friend in alcohol. The bottle began to numb Ferd's feelings of grief and failure. Alcohol provided a respite to his physical and emotional pain. At this time, there were no support groups. No Alcoholics Anonymous. He found solace in drink, despite the fact that Prohibition in South Dakota extended for over forty-five years and was full fledged from 1917 until 1935. Across the country, practically in another world, in New York, Bill Wilson was writing a book.

Did this motherless family find support? Did Ferd receive help from the parish priest or neighbors? Did he ask for help from anything other than a bottle? Neither Mom nor her brothers ever described Grandpa as an alcoholic. Never. Mom did mention his eyebrow, though. "When Dad's eyebrow rose ...," she'd say, her voice trailing off. She never shared what happened when the eyebrow rose. I never asked.

About the time without her mother, Mom told me, "I believe after Mom died, she watched over us. Protected us." Perhaps. Once she said she believed her mom came back for her dad, "as if to protect us." She never elaborated. I never pushed for further explanation. I knew better.

The Brauns' sadness, or what Mom called the "Tracy Curse," continued. Three months after the death of his wife, the man who had been burned early in their marriage while attempting to stave off their own house fire, who had worked to break the prairie sod to feed his family, who was devastated by the death of his wife and the mother of his six children, and who began struggling with alcohol, was killed.

Mom struggled to tell the story of how he died. "After several tanks exploded by the railroad tracks in Lemmon, smoke rolled; the smell was stifling as the entire town came to see the inferno. In the chaos, a train was blasting through, unaware of the fire. Dad was standing near the railroad track. Due to the noise surrounding him, he did not hear the approaching train. Bill Stoick, a friend, saw the ominous threat, but Dad was oblivious to the reality. Bill ran to save Dad. Both were hit. Dad's legs were severed, and he died a few hours later. We heard Dad's screams of pain as we ran to the hospital. Doc Totten, the local savior and one of Ferd's longtime friends, attempted to save him. Doc Totten said, 'Ferd, I will take away the pain.'"

Mom's tears told of the pain of the moment that changed the Braun children, of Doc's assurance that he'd take the pain away. He did. With morphine. It did not quicken his death, rather it provided relief from the inevitable. The morphine stopped the screams. Ferd lived a few hours. His children sat in the stark hospital waiting room, anxious to hear word of their father's fate. Doc Totten delivered the grim news. This last tragic fire took Ferd's life. Bill survived, without his legs.

Mom felt the depth of her father's death in multiple ways. Whenever she talked of him, she'd pause, get a faraway look in her eyes. One story she often told us when we were young about her father was different from the rest. We, her three oldest daughters, called it The Story of the Yellow Dress. Mom's eyes filled with tears when she spoke.

Mom began. "'Dad,' I begged. 'Please? Please?' I pleaded with him in our little house, no longer a home without Mom's presence. I was a teenager. Mom had died a couple months before. Walking with my cousin, I had spotted a yellow dress in The Golden Rule, a local store. I wanted it for the upcoming dance. Forlorn, defeated, missing Mom at such important junctures, I just begged him. Dad raised his eyes to meet mine. 'LaVerna,' he said. 'I don't have the money. If I did, I would buy it.' When I protested, he said emphatically again, 'I don't have the money.'

"As the only girl, Dad spoiled me. He always gave in. This time he didn't. Anger spilled from my mouth. If Dad would not grant my wishes, I would run away. Leave home. I packed my few belongings and went to live with my friend." Tears ran down Mom's face as she continued the story. "Within hours of my move, I was notified Dad was injured in an accident, a fire. I ran to the hospital. My brothers, one playing a baseball game, the others playing or working, came running as the town people notified us. We heard the screams as we ran up the steps to the hospital. Dad's screams. He died shortly after the boys and I arrived at the hospital. Now alone. No mother. No father. We went home. I opened the door. I gasped. The crisp, bright yellow dress hung on the doorsill. I never had the opportunity to say I was sorry. I never wore the yellow dress."

The guilt remained. It was one of several pervasiveness sources of guilt throughout my mother's life. Ultimately, guilt affected not only her life, but also the lives of her children. No one ever said if Grandpa Ferd had been drinking on the day of his death.

Mom's journal is unrelenting. "Mom and Dad dead. It was 1935, the Depression. No money. No crops. No feed for the animals. The entire country suffered. The six of us moved to the little house Grandma Tracy had given our family after losing the café and before Mom died. The six of us made a promise. We will stay together. No matter what."

Mom continued, "I found a job at the local café. Lawrence, now married, worked in a store with Carl. The little boys sold the *Grit* newspaper." They somehow endured the winter and the next year of school. Mom's only reference to the next three years was, "We barely survived."

The journal entries became more hopeful. "Dad left a small insurance policy. I received $150. Taking $90, I moved with the little boys, Ferdie and Wally, to Aberdeen, South Dakota, to attend Beauty School. The older boys were now on their own. I found work at a café to pay our board and room. The boys found another paper route. We managed until I completed beauty school."

The journal continued, accounting for the whereabouts of the siblings. "Ferdie returned to Lemmon, lived with Carl, now married, worked as a meat cutter at the Golden Rule Store. Jim lived and worked with Uncle Jim Tracy on a farm north of Lemmon. Lawrence and his new wife, Edna, moved to Arizona, and he worked in a mine. Wally, now a junior in high school, moved with me as I began my career as a beautician in Sioux Falls, South Dakota."

Sioux Falls was where LaVerna Katherine Braun met, fell in love with, and married Alfred John Sanow. The journal does not cite date or place. Or much of anything else about their love story. Only that it happened.

In 1940, the war broke out. The Braun boys served: Jim in the army, Carl in the Coast Guard, Ferd in the marine corp, and Lawrence as a cook in the Merchant Marines. Mom and Dad, now married, and Wally, the youngest of the Brauns and at that time a senior in high school, moved to Montrose, South Dakota.

Since his older brothers had joined the armed services, the baby Braun brother wanted to join, too, as in the famous story of the Sullivan brothers. He was seventeen years old, too young to enlist on his own. Mom and Dad reluctantly signed the papers that gained him admittance. Wally enlisted in the navy, where he finished school.

Mom, a rabid supporter of veterans, often said of the "boys" and their years of service, "My brothers returned physically from the service, but not emotionally." She was right. They all struggled at different times with drinking. It was genetically and situationally influenced. Mom loved, protected, and excused any bad behavior throughout her brothers' lives. For most of her brother's deaths, she was present when they died, burying them with their families with dignity. As for me, I deeply loved all of the uncles I came to know.

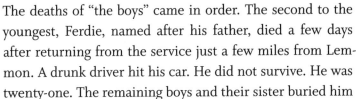

The deaths of "the boys" came in order. The second to the youngest, Ferdie, named after his father, died a few days after returning from the service just a few miles from Lemmon. A drunk driver hit his car. He did not survive. He was twenty-one. The remaining boys and their sister buried him alongside his parents in Green Hill Cemetery in Lemmon.

Lawrence, after losing six-year-old daughter Muriel to drowning, went to the bottle. Alcohol numbed the pain. Some years later, Mom sent for Lawrence and his wife, Edna, with the intent of helping the already-struggling marriage. During the visit home, Lawrence died at our home of a massive heart attack. Mom said, "He came home to die among those who loved him." I knew she was right. He was forty-three.

The youngest of the Braun boys, Wallace (my oldest brother was his name sake), a Korean War veteran, struggled with the disease of alcoholism for years, dying at forty-three from complications of alcoholism and cancer. Mom was with him.

Jim, married to Viola, a woman who became my closest and dearest aunt, fathered five children. During a night of drinking, he was stabbed thirty-one times. He survived. The knife was wielded by an African American man. Mom never forgot the color of the man who hurt her brother. The prejudice resurrected throughout her life. Retired after thirty-five years of working in the gold mine in Lead, Jim died of multiple medical complications.

Carl, married to Aunt Vi's sister, Dorothy, provided for five children. Jim and Carl, after years of drinking, finally stopped, and lived long, fruitful lives. Mom visited Jim shortly before his death and was with Carl when he died. With their families, she buried all five of her brothers. They lovingly called her Sis. She called them "the boys," something that always reminded me of Father Flannigan, who opened and founded a home for orphaned, abandoned, and often-neglected boys in 1917. He called it Boy's Town. Father Flannigan once told the story of one of "his boys" as saying, when carrying one of his new brothers on his back, "He ain't heavy, Father; he's my brother." Mom loved the motto. With her brothers, she lived it.

Chapter 3

This is the woman, now widowed, who smiled and said to her four unsuspecting children, "I have a surprise for you!"

"What?" we asked, jumping, excited, surrounding her in our cozy Montrose kitchen.

"I am going on a date."

The first one after Dad's death.

A knock at the door. Mom moved toward it. She opened the door. There he stood. Harry Irwin Kittelson. Tall, lean, in khaki pants and with a gentle face. Mom had grown up with him. We children had never met him; it was our first meeting. We ran to hide in the stairwell. The four Sanow children crowded under the stairs, peaked out of the crack in the door as he came to court, bearing gifts. Our eyes popped out. Not at him. It was the gift. Gum. Bubble gum. For four young children, it was love at first sight. It was total acceptance of the man about to become our father and it was based on Bazooka bubble gum, most of which ended up in our hair, bedding, and bowels.

Mom was to know love again. So, too, her four children. Harry, a thirty-six-year-old bachelor, was about to enter a ready-made family and become a father. He dated all five of us. Miraculously, he married all five of us. The Bazooka bubble gum helped. Things were never the same for him, or us.

Romanticism was not our new dad's strong suit. Pragmatism was. His proposal, written in a love letter, went something like this: "I don't have anything, but maybe if we pooled our interests, a home and family could be established." He said later, "There seemed to be no disagreement to this." On July 23, 1953, they married at Saint Patrick's rectory with the support and love of the entire community of Montrose, including my biological father's family.

Harry Irwin Kittelson. He came from humble immigrant Norwegian homesteaders. His beloved mother, Ida, died in his teen years. He was left with a father who, even before his wife's death, was void of emotion and who remained empty of them after. Raised on the prairie of the Dakotas, Harry Irwin Kittelson, however, became a man of extraordinary integrity.

Grandpa was not pleased about Dad marrying a Catholic woman who happened to be a Democrat and who had four children. But Grandpa received a package deal. So did we. I referred to it as our New Deal, coined from FDR's moniker. His part of the deal was a daughter-in-law and four ready-made grandchildren. Our part was a dad and a grandpa. I know we liked our deal better than he liked his. I loved Grandpa Kittelson, even though he was at times a "crabby paddy."

Ma and Pa Kettle were characters in a popular film series at the time we married our new dad. The hillbilly couple with fifteen children famously played out their antics on the big screen. Everyone laughed. When people saw our family coming down the road, they had the same response: laughter and a few headshakes. They saw this longtime-available bachelor married to this woman with "all those kids." They called them Ma and Pa Kettle and us kids all the little pots and pans.

"LaVone, stop." Our new father reached for the pop bottle, poised in midair; its target, my head. We were on what we called our honeymoon for six. Vonnie was chasing me with a pop bottle. As our new father prepared for his first night of wedded bliss, Dad was saving the life of his new daughter. It was not to be the last time. He also was teaching two sisters. Vonnie and I sat on a chair with this task: "Think about how you will love your sister."

Vonnie and me. Two blondes. Vonnie, taller. I, always physically smaller. We were inseparable in everything. We even shared seats. "You sit on this side. I will sit on this side," I instructed my little sister, fourteen months younger, after we had rushed to the bathroom. When we were little, it took too much time for both of us to go to the bathroom. We had important things to do. Like play. So I came up with one of our many brilliant ideas: to sit down at the same time. Share the seat. It was always like that. Sharing and fighting and sharing again.

Our brilliant ideas often came in bundles. Slugger, our golden, gentle cocker spaniel would just stand there as we bathed and wiped him off with Mom's new blanket. Hair got all over. Fearing retribution, we stuffed Mom's new blanket in the far reaches of the porch closet.

My favorite game was one we made up. It was called Roy Rogers and Dale Evans. I was Roy Rogers, the timeless cowboy. My sister, Vonnie, was Dale Evans, his wife. We used the big gray gas tank for our horses, Trigger and Buttermilk; the tank loops held our ropes. "Gitty up!" we yelled as we made believe our big, fat, gray steeds actually listened. Old Yeller, which we based on the Disney movie about the loving dog in a pioneer family, was another game we played.

We shared and stole each other's clothes. Fought about chores. She threw everything under the bed or in a drawer, stuffed things in the closet. I cleaned under the beds, made order to the drawers and closets. I felt constant frustration with her when it came to cleaning and doing the dishes. She hated anything domestic. I loved it.

We shared the same room and bed. Every night as we got under the covers, we'd fight over the space, but by the time we fell asleep, her leg was always draped over mine.

And in the night, she sucked her thumb. I sucked the back of my hand. We tried to stop. I suggested, "Vonnie, let's paint our thumb and back of our hand with white shoe polish." It was another one of my brilliant ideas. She covered her thumb and I covered my hand prior to going to bed on night. In the morning, white shoe polish covered my mouth, Vonnie's, too. Then I had another brilliant idea. "If the white didn't work, how about black polish?" I do not know how we quit. But we did.

She loved to fight. Physical fights. And she was tough. Really tough. Always taller, stronger, faster than I was, I was no match. Instead of fighting, I liked to talk things through. She didn't. So she was constantly getting us in situations. "You are the older one, Annetta," Mom often said. "You know better. Vonnie just follows what you do." This was just one of the many misperceptions Mom held about me. And about Vonnie.

I spent a great deal of time trying to talk to people out of beating the hell out of my sister because of something she said. At those times, she exhausted me. And punishment always followed. I never understood how I ended up being punished for what Vonnie started.

Then there was sweet Karren, our older sister and gentle advisor. She nurtured her two younger siblings and everyone with whom she came into contact. Wally, our brother, and Karren had a close relationship because of their birth order, but there was more. Karren served as Wally's confidant their entire lives.

Growing up, Karren was the tallest in her class, but she graduated one of the shortest. As a child, she won a beauty contest. As an adolescent, she suffered through a horrible case of acne. "I am so ugly," she said one morning when I found her crying in front of the mirror getting ready for school. "No, Karren; you are the most beautiful woman in the world," I told her. And I meant it. In my mind's eye, I can still see her crying as she tried to cover the blemishes with makeup. Mom gently worked with her, drawing on her professional skin-care expertise and consoling and encouraging her.

Anyone with a heart loved Karren. One of the most popular girls in our school, she was crowned homecoming queen, was a cheerleader and friend. None of the accolades went to her head. Even then, she was one of the finest human beings I will ever know.

"You are now the man of the house. You must take care of your mother and sisters," a well-meaning person told my brother, Wally, a few days after Dad's death. Wally, the oldest and only boy. He was eight years old at the time. The message was passed along unbeknownst to his three sisters. He took that charge seriously. To us sisters, Wally was God. Our protector. He was always there. As teenage girls, we depended on Wally as our "birth control." He protected us, was extremely strict.

He was also extremely encouraging. "Annetta did it! Look you guys. Annetta did it," my brother yelled one day when I was about to take part in a rite of passage. The sun reflected brightly off the gray trailer as we stood on the plank sidewalk. It was summertime in South Dakota. Someone had distributed Bazooka bubble gum. Well practiced because of all the bubble gum we kids had received during Mom and Dad's courtship, I had attempted, but failed miserably, to blow a bubble on numerous occasions. This was always to the great delight of my siblings, who laughed as the sticky goo fell over my face time and time again.

As I began to blow and blow, I pledge that this day was to be like no other. And then there it was: a full-scale bubble. In spontaneous combustion, a chorus of cheers and clapping ignited that little piece of land in the Dakota's. I had arrived. It was hard to know who was more excited, my brother or me. God, I loved my brother. I truly thought he was God. We always knew he would be there.

"I will take care of this," Wally assured his three sisters one day after being thrown down by Hugo, the bully of our neighborhood.

"He took the scooter, Wally." Karren reported. She was referring to our sacred, rusted, red scooter. "We have to give him fifty cents or he will keep it," Karren cried.

Vonnie and I shook our heads in unison. Instead of running the other way, our brother came up with a plan. "Run when I grab the scooter," Wally told us.

"What?" we asked in unison.

"He'll kill you!" Karren said, echoing what was in both Vonnie's and my mind. We knew the bully was much bigger than Wally.

"When I drop the fifty cents in Hugo's hand, run!" he repeated

"What?" we girls asked again. The risk was great. And anyway, where in God's green earth was Wally going to find fifty cents?

The foursome approached Hugo. "I want fifty cents and you can have your crummy scooter back," the bully said.

Wally, with his three petrified sisters behind him, confidently said, "No problem. You put your hand out; I will place my hand on the scooter for the exchange." The hands went out. When Wally dropped what Hugo anticipated to be a fifty-cent piece in Hugo's hand, we ran. Wally had really given Hugo a rock. As I ran, I looked back. Hugo stood there with his mouth open looking at the rock. And Wally had the scooter.

Yet another memory. The ball burned my small hand as he threw it to me and I caught it. I said nothing. We were playing ball in the vacant lot across the alley from our house. He asked me to catch a baseball so he could practice his skills. His throw was strong. My hand burned. The ball came too fast for a small child. But I didn't mind. I was playing catch with my brother. Even as a small girl, I knew that the pain was insignificant compared to the joy of being with my hero.

With no real help from me, Wally became an outstanding athlete, participating in baseball, basketball, football, and track. He played on the first state basketball team to come from our little school. All of this came after the bullies in our high school threw the bike Dad had bought Wally before his death into the little lake outside of town and unmercifully teased him about taking piano lessons. We pulled the bike out of the lake. But he stopped playing piano.

Always a hero to his sisters, Wally harbored his own private shadows. A poem he wrote in high school may have been an indication of what was to come.

TRACK
Track, Track, Track.
How I hate that!
Track, Track, track.
Get off my back—Track!

Blues, Blues, Blues.
How I hate track shoes!
Booze, Booze, Booze.
I'd rather do that, than lose.

Run, Run, Run.
Till the whole darn day is done.
Puff, Puff, Puff.
If you don't do that—Shev (the coach) will gruff.
  —Wally Sanow

Chapter 4

Our mom's new marriage necessitated our move to McIntosh, South Dakota, one of a multitude of small communities built along Highway 12 and called railroad towns. Prior to the marriage, our new dad worked with the Corson County Highway Department. The little town sat on the wide-open prairies surrounded by golden grasses in the late summer, stubble fields covered with snow in the winter, rolling, beautiful emerald fields in the spring, and yellow grains waiting to be harvested in the fall.

The plains of the Dakotas. In the depth of winter, some people call it tundra. We who lived there knew better.

Main Street, the only paved city road in town, hosted multiple businesses. Highway 12 also meandered through the north side of the tiny town. It, too, was paved. Soon after we moved to McIntosh, the new Highway 12 was built two blocks from the old one. The new road skirted the town, taking much needed revenue with it.

In the 1950s, approximately five hundreds souls resided in and around McIntosh, named after Alexander McIntosh, an engineer, who with his brother laid the road through the fledgling town. The county seat of Corson County, McIntosh was founded in 1908 and bordered the Standing Rock Indian Reservation. It still does. Sitting Bull lived on this land.

In its early days, McIntosh was a thriving railroad town, with cafés and three mercantile stores. The only residents noted in the early history were the white people, their German, Russian, and Scandinavian descent dotted with a sundry mixture of other nationalities.

The land on which the town developed was purchased from Joseph Archambault, a Native American, a man whose identity the town's history tellers have often neglected to mention. But the facts stand. Through treaties from the government, Joseph received an allotment of 640 aces and sold it to the Milwaukee Railroad in 1907 to establish a town. The city of McIntosh was plotted on this land. Joseph purchased back three lots, building a general store, along with one in the nearby Indian town of Bullhead. He also built the Standing Rock Hotel, noted as the finest, most up-to-date hotel between Miles City, Montana, and Aberdeen, South Dakota. It burned in 1915.

Joseph served in public office in a myriad of capacities. Yet no one mentions Joseph. I had never heard of him during my nine years of public education in the local school, although others outside of the Dakotas recognized our town, and its Native American roots, as the little city on the prairies connected to Standing Rock Reservation. Outsiders like prospector George M. Bailey of Rochester, New York, called it the "gateway to the great Standing Rock Reservation." The locals felt differently.

Even as a child, I felt the Native Americans were mistreated, although I didn't understand all of the nuances then as I do today. I just knew they were treated differently than white people. Abject poverty surrounded them. Engulfed them.

"Hey, ye, ye, ye. Hey, ye, ye, ye." I grew up hearing the mesmerizing beat of the drum, the deep, melodic, guttural, wailing sound of the singers. Powwows, pageants of sound and color, were the gatherings of Indian people. Uneducated about the ceremonies and culture, I did not then understand their underlying traditions, the sacredness. I was ignorant of the terms and meaning of the Fancy Dance, of the traditional dancers and grass dancers, of jingle dresses and fancy shawls. But even then I loved the drumming, its earthiness and beauty. And I loved the unique humor of the native people.

When relatives from other parts of the country came to visit, they often exhibited unfounded, unrealistic fear when we took them for visits to the small Native American communities of Bullhead, Wakapla, and Little Eagle. But even my experience was naïve. While I grew up knowing the names Sitting Bull and Sacagawea, I knew nothing of their legacy or the backstory of their plight.

Our second dad knew the truth. He knew the truth about the culture and shared it with us in his actions. He took us to Powwows. The Indian towns. He sat and visited. He also understood their humor and their pain. Although sometimes frustrated, Dad loved the native people. And they loved him.

On the reservation near our home, one boy stood out. He was black. His name was Homer. Homer White Buffalo. Later, I found out his middle name. Joseph.

～

"No." Mom threw the paring knife and the potato she was peeling into the sink. My head jerked back. Setting the table for supper, I was young.

"C'mon, Mom," Wally, my brother, pleaded. Mom was inflexible, angry. "Mom, he has nowhere to go. Please let him eat supper with us."

"Absolutely not." Her voice was tense. I looked out into the backyard. The boy was bouncing the basketball on the plank sidewalk. He looked different. I had never seen someone with black skin.

"I will not have a black person in my house," Mom said, emphatically.

I was mad at Mom's words. I thought, "Why is she so mad?" Too young to respond, I knew if I said something, punishment would follow. You NEVER responded by revealing your feelings to Mom. She considered it talking back. It was completely unacceptable behavior. With Mom, Wally could get away with it.

Defeated this time, Wally went back to his new friend. But not before he grabbed a slice of bread from the table. I slipped Wally a freshly baked chocolate chip cookie from the side cupboard for his new friend. His name was Homer.

I was only a fourth grader and couldn't make sense of Mom's reaction. I can still hear the metal from the parry knife hit the side of the porcelain sink. It was a defining moment in my life.

Later, not only did Homer eat at our table, but he also slept in our beds. In fact, he became like a son to Mom and Dad. He also entered the heart of Mom's fourth child: he was my first love. The cookie was a precursor.

~

Unaware of the true implications of bigotry, alcoholism, poverty, or what was happening around us, we blithely moved through the innocence of childhood. From our vantage point, our town was a place of peace. We played kick the can, hide and seek, and cowboys and Indians all day, every day. We played Roy Rogers and Dale Evans. Roy Rogers. My first male role model other than my dads. The next was John Kennedy; he was running for senate. I was drawn to him at an early age.

Vonnie and I, never far from one another, shared a bedroom and bed not just with one another, but also with Karren, at least until she became a teenager. That's when Dad said, "Karren, you get your own room," as he completed rooms in the basement for the two older children. She had pinups of Ricky Nelson, Sandra Dee, and Bobby Darin on the walls.

When she asked, "Do you two want to sleep with me?" we flew to her bed. It was like a dream. We lay there with our big sister, listening to KOMA in Oklahoma City. Life was never better. The sister slumber parties were an opportunity to plan our futures. Make promises.

Karren. Our protector. Our guide.

~~~

Every Saturday night, less than a block from our home, it was twenty-five cents for a movie and ten cents for popcorn. The Lyric Theater blared phonograph music from the small opening in the projector room, calling us with the words, "Wonder, wonder who, who wrote the book of love?" The music floated through the air, along with the wonderful aroma of corn popping. My sisters, brother, and I sat like millionaires on wooden seats, smelling the years of entertainment in the musty air.

Saturday night, the country people joined the town people, visiting, shopping, and walking the streets, while the young people watched the movie. Others sat in the numerous bars.

We listened to the Lone Ranger on the radio. We had no TV. The three of us sang, "Catch a falling star and put it in your pocket, save it for a rainy day" and "I hear the cottonwoods whisperin above, Tammy, Tammy, Tammy's in love." Nothing seemed to be a struggle. We were ignorant of prejudices, politics, or starving children. If people were hungry, folks, including my own, generally fed them. (Homer proved to be a temporary exception.)

The closest thing to our really knowing hunger was when Dad threatened, "Eat your food, or I will take you over to Nick Blankets and bring his children here to eat. They would appreciate the food." Nick Blanket was a Native American man with many children and no money. Nick lived a Lakota tradtion, called "Mitakuye Oyasin" it means "All our relatives." He took in the people of his tribe because they *all* are relatives. Dad respected Nick because he was so generous.

~~~~~

Our town was a place of peace, serenity, and security. You were never alone. Through the windows, mothers watched one another's children. The kids didn't know it, though. But it meant that we got away with nothing. We tried. Tried to slip to the drugstore to sip a drink from the soda fountain, or to Ed Robb's candy store for a piece of penny candy or a five-cent pack of sunflower seeds. If you achieved such a feat, you felt as though you had died and gone to heaven. Since stealing was generally out, we sold pop bottles we found in the alleys to get spending money for candy. The glass bottles brought three cents apiece; once, the total went to a short-lived, whopping five cents.

We had neighborhood arguments, challenging one another with "Who threw the rock?" or "Who took the ball?" We made mud pies and decorated them with pods from caragana bushes or with pink, yellow, or white hollyhock flowers. We dried our pies in the sun. We presented dandelions bouquets to our mothers.

We attempted to roller skate on the crumbling sidewalks, tightening our skates with medal keys and uttering prayers that God would keep them tight on our saddle shoes. When they didn't, we skinned our knees. We played in the vacant lot by our house: baseball, softball, or whatever ball we could find. Sometimes we had no ball, so we used a stick and a rock.

In the spring, we ate wild onions and stunk up the whole classroom. We culprits were never punished, because it would have shut down the school. We all ate them.

Life was filled with swinging on homemade swings and playing seven-up on the side of any building with a flat surface. It was heaven.

Mom began to wear what we thought looked like a tent. On November 13, 1954, the tent emptied and out came our little sister, Mary Katherine Kittelson. For us, it was like the second coming of Jesus Christ. Everyone was ecstatic. A baby sister! However, with Mary came an ear infection. Dad or Mom walked the floor every night trying to keep her from crying. Vonnie and I cried when Mary cried. We felt bad for our helpless, tiny sister.

Dad made up a song during those long nights: "She's a bungee baby. She's a bungee girl." He sang it over and over. The man's patience was incredible. I don't know if Mary ever fell asleep with Dad's singing, but Vonnie and I sure did. Dad had a beautiful voice.

John and Irene Erz. Tony and Leona Senftner. Marge and Barney Katus. John and Gen Nicksic. Alvin and Verna Jacobs. Sid and Helen Hourigan. These were families important to our lives. Lifelong friends. All but the Katus were Catholic. Nevertheless, "The Katuses," Mom would say, "are God-fearing, good people." She was right.

My siblings and I spent our summers playing Red Rover, tag, or ante, ante over with their children, all of whom were my best friends: DeLaine, Nick, Bill, Mary Ann, and Jimmy Erz.

"Jimmy, you are so funny," I would say with a giggle. Jimmy and I spent many days together, since Mom, Irene, Dad, and John were often together. Jimmy had mischievous eyes and a distinctive giggle of his own. He made me laugh. His giggle started in his toes and radiated throughout his little body. I loved it. We'd sit on a massive tire-turned-sandbox and just giggle for hours. He'd start it. I'd follow suit. I loved Jimmy and his giggle.

Like Grandma Bessie, Mom made choke cherry jelly with the tart fruit, and we'd slather it onto pieces of her freshly made bread. The choke cherry tree stood in our back yard. The tree served us kids well, providing us with a climbing post that allowed us to scurry across the garage roof so Mom couldn't see—or catch—us.

Coal heated most homes in those days. We held sacred the times we spent riding with Dad in the old, deep green International pickup truck to Firesteel, South Dakota, to pick up coal. Once home, we'd shovel it into the coal shoot, concluding the day with black covering our faces. Homes were often covered with a gray film that resulted from stoking the furnace, removing the ashes, and the major project of removing the large clinkers, the remnants of the burnt coal. It was back-breaking work, but Dad did it without complaint.

LaVerna's Beauty Shop, later called The Fashion Shop, opened in our home. If Mom was to have a beauty shop, Dad wanted it in our home. He did not want Mom working outside the home. The issue was what Dad would call "a bone of contention." Such "bones of contention" showed up several times during their marriage. They almost always had to do with finances, which in those days were impacted by the Depression.

Their different approaches to the family budget manifested in contradictory ways. Mom was a spender, Dad a saver. Better put, he was frugal. Dad built the salon on the front porch. Later, Mom moved it a little over twenty-five miles east to McLaughlin, South Dakota.

Hers was a diversified salon. She styled, permed, and cut hair, and provided facials, pedicures, and manicures. She had mastered beautification. I loved working at Mom's beauty shops. My job was to clean and sterilize combs and brushes, sweep hair, and wipe counters. Mom liked it when people remarked what a good helper I was.

I also watched Mom minister to the women of the community with her shears and her ears. She was good. Beauty salons are notorious places for gossip, but she stopped the gossip midstream with remarks like, "I have a house filled with children and but for the grace of God..." The gossip would stop. The gossiper "got" the message. With her professional ethics intact, Mom had an even stronger personal moral code.

"Fire! The school!"

People were yelling. The news went through town like a wildfire. Everyone was running toward our school. Mom grabbed our small hands. The smell of smoke was faint at first, but grew stronger as we walked, then ran, toward the school. I was afraid. The flames raged as we stood a short block away. Mom kept making the sign of the cross. Tears running down her face, she said, "Oh, dear God." Over and over again. On July 25, 1955, our school burned just before the beginning of my first grade.

The community watched helplessly as the 1921 school went up in flames. Sam Klaudt, our sainted janitor, had just finished waxing the floors when a spark apparently escaped from the burn barrel, a container in which he commonly burned trash, and came in through an open window. The entire town watched, helpless.

I remember crying. For me, the only educational experience in the old school was to be kindergarten with Marge Katus, our teacher. It took two years to complete the new school. By then, I was a third grader. I loved our new school, with its bright new walls, glistening floors, huge gym with a stage and maroon-and-gold curtains monogrammed with the letters MHS. It was exquisite. Other than the bars, it was the center of our little town.

"Everyone in," Dad called. I scrambled to sit next to Dad in the pickup. I loved sitting next to Dad. It gave me a sense of safety. Wally, Karren, and I filled the cab. "We're off!" Dad said. Mom waved as the motor purred. In reality, the truck, which we called "Old Green," made a deafening racket. Forty miles later, Dad dropped us off in front of Saint Mary's convent in Lemmon, South Dakota. Honoring the desire of our first father and the presence of the piano in our front room, Dad encouraged us to "play nice."

Buoyed by the ride, I climbed the steps and rang the doorbell of the expansive mansion. My heart skipped a beat when the door opened. Standing in front of me was a woman in long black dress and starched white face. A nun. It was my first experience of nuns and would not be the last. Next to God and priests, nuns, I thought, and was taught, were the next holiest people on the face of the earth. I was in awe and scared to death. Petrified is a better description.

While I was patiently being taught piano at the convent, Wally and Karren received their lessons at Saint Mary's school, affiliated with St. Mary's Church. The church sat beside the convent and school. It was the same church and school attended by Mom and her brothers. The Braun children had received sacraments at Saint Mary's Church. They had prayed there at the funerals of their beloved parents.

My lessons occurred on an upright piano, similar to the one delivered to our home in Montrose and that moved with us the four hundred miles to McIntosh. Sister Michael was my piano teacher. A restless spirit, she tried to be patient with me. Sometimes it worked. Most of the nuns had significant patience. These piano lessons began the incalculable impact of the Benedictines on my life.

Later this restless spirit left her religious order prior even to the massive exodus of religious and priests in the 1970s.

Dad picked us up an hour later, giving each of us a dime to shop at the local Ben Franklin store. The lessons were hell.

The dime was heaven. Returning home Saturday afternoon, we began to prepare for Sunday. One ritual was the application of shoe polish to our black-and-white saddle shoes, an act of total futility that involved trying not to get the black polish on the white leather or the white polish on the black leather.

Confessions at Saint Bonaventure were also part of our weekly preparations. We went whether we committed a sin or not. I always had. Some of the confessions were at Mom's discretion, like on the day Vonnie and I played "going to the store" in Mom's blue '49 Chevy by pretending to drive the car. The adventure lasted only until our little sister, Mary, a little over a year old and playing the roll of our baby, pushed down the lock on the door on the one-hundred-degree day. Mom had to break the window to recover her. It wasn't pretty. Mom said I had to go to confession. Off to the confessional I went.

I knelt with great piety and fervor, examining my conscience. It was the same litany as always: I had hit my sisters, said bad words, and didn't listen to Mom and Dad. I never hit my brother. Only my sisters, and really, only Vonnie. Father told me those were venial sins. Not really bad. However, they were not really good.

Mortal sins were the big ones. The greatest sins of all were stealing, killing, and adultery. I had no idea what adultery was, but it sounded bad. The closest thing I had to understanding killing was from the newsreels that played before the movie at the Lyric when the cowboys and Indian chased each other. We never saw them dead, though: only dust and smoke.

What prepared me for being so practiced in the confessional, other than having some guilt, occurred when I was in the first grade. My First Communion teacher, Irene Erz,

Jimmy's mom and a saint in our town and parish, taught us about God, sin, and the seven sacraments, two of which, Holy Communion and confession, this little group of first graders were about to receive. Mom and Irene were my first teachers in the faith, followed by our parish priest, Father Joseph O'Rourke.

He taught me how to confess. Boy, did he teach me how to confess.

"I stole Black Jack gum," I said, my seven-year-old voice trembling as I prepared for my First Communion in the screened confessional. A short time before the rites of first confession and First Communion, I had stolen a pack of Black Jack gum from Senftner's grocery store when my mom and Leona, one of the owners, were visiting. So easy. Sin, I later found out, is like that. It tricks you. I quietly flipped the glorious blue-and-black licorice gum from the recess of the candy counter to my hand to the pocket of my pants.

Eating it later was like a mystical experience. I thought that I was pretty smart, until Father O'Rourke's instruction for our First Communion. Then when I confessed, he told me, "Say three Hail Mary's and make restitution," from the other side of the screen. I had no idea what restitution meant. It sounded ominous.

Father O'Rourke must have realized the word was confusing for a first grader. "Pay back the person who owned the Black Jack gum," he instructed. It was a major dilemma. The five cents it took to buy a pack and pay it back was out of reach for a seven-year-old child. There was never any change lying around the bedroom I shared with my two sisters. Then I thought, "Pop bottles! I will find and sell pop bottles!"

That common source of cash for children. If I could secure and then sell two pop bottles, receiving three cents apiece, I would keep myself from going to the pits of hell and losing the state of grace that apparently was necessary to receive my First Holy Communion.

Lucky for me, I found and sold two pop bottles. I then took the nickel and returned to the scene of the crime, Tony and Leona's grocery store. Tony and Leona Senftner were more than local grocers; they were family friends. Bill, their second son, was one of my friends. I had committed a crime within our family of friends. Bill never knew about it; we became boyfriend and girlfriend in second or third grade. He later proposed to me in our large tire sandbox. I think we were eight. Significant things occurred on that tire sandbox.

When I took the six cents I had gotten from the pop bottles and pushed the shiny nickel over the edge of the wooden counter, I held tight to the penny in my hand. At least, I thought, I can get a piece of penny candy after I returned to a state of grace, typical of the mind of a criminal. When I had made my restitution, relief washed over me. "I am free," I thought. "I paid it back. Now I can make my First Holy Communion!"

In May of 1956, at Saint Bonaventure, our little, white, clapboard, steeple-on-the-top church, I received the Body and Blood of our Lord, with appropriate piety, alongside Jimmy Erz, my processional partner. Somehow, we refrained from giggling.

Our Catholic tradition teaches that the host is transfigured into the Body of Christ at the most sacred moment in the Mass. And although I had made restitution for my sinful theft, it was lodged in my seven-year-old, scrupulous mind, and followed me until I was twenty seven years old, when I made amends to Leona for the theft; Tony, by that time was dead. I told her I was sorry. Even with restitution, the guilt still bothered me. Catholic conscience comes early, stays late.

~~~~~

"Oh, dear God," Mom cried. Uncharacteristically, Dad had arrived home from his county roadwork at midday. He told Mom that Jimmy Erz had been dragged by one of the family horses. Mom broke down and kept saying through her tears, "Poor Irene, John."

I was scared. "Jimmy, what? Jimmy? What does this mean?" I thought. I could not talk.

Shortly after our First Communion, my best friend Jimmy Erz, Irene and John's son, was dragged to his death by a horse. For his funeral, we again wore our First Communion dresses. Jimmy's gentle mother, Irene, and kind-hearted father, John, sat in the front row. Jimmy's First Communion class sat in the front row on the opposite side. I cried.

It was the second time I had seen the box. This time, I was tall enough to see Jimmy's body. He just lay there, meticulous in his First Communion suit. No giggles, no mischievous smile. I felt sick to my stomach. He had the same suit on he wore a few weeks before walking beside me in the procession. To this day, I can still hear his distinctive giggle. To this day, Jimmy's death makes me cry.

Catholic traditions surrounded our life. The May crowning of Mary was held the first Sunday of May. According to Mom, May, the month of the Blessed Virgin Mary, was the most important month of the year. In later years, I understood mother's devotion to Mary. It came from the death of her mother. The Blessed Mother filled the bill. Mom held her tight all her life. Although her devotion to Mary sometimes drove me nuts, I have no doubt that it saved my mother's life more than once.

We sang "Tantrum Ergo Sacramentum" along with "Holy God, We Praise Thy Name." Benediction was held every Sunday night, with the divine praises and incense; depending on the priest, the clouds of smoke sent us into fits of coughing.

There were dark sides of congregational life at that time, however. Some involved the church trustees. These were always men designated to take care of certain aspects of church business. At one point, a priest who had the courage to address the booming bar business in our town found himself without heat. The trustees had shut it off. "They are going to kill him if they continue," I heard Mom say in muted tones to Dad. She thought it was cruel. One angry lady actually urinated on the priest's shoes.

Not long after, Father returned to his ancestral home for a vacation and died of a heart attack. When Mom received the call from his family, she turned from the phone and said, "God took him back to die surrounded by people who loved him." It was not the only time cruelty was exercised against the parish priest. Cruel people reside even in churches.

Another significant event occurred among some of the more prominent people in the community. Mom and Dad were invited to join a local group of couples that called itself the Key Club. Thinking it was a group of civic-minded people doing good things, they soon found out the meaning of the name. When the group got together, the men's keys were thrown in a circle. The women each picked up a set and the newly paired-up couples . . . well, you can imagine.

Mom and Dad boycotted and were never to be accepted by the group again. They didn't care. It was one of the many times they took the high ground.

Fear in church, mixed with awe, was a constant companion for me as a child. There was no talking, no whispering, and no fun in church. It was serious. Sacred. Holy. I watched my parents kneel, along with everyone else. If you rested on your rump, you weren't as holy as the rest. No one ever told me that; I just thought it.

~

"Silent Night" played softly from the music box under the rotating cardboard scene of one shepherd and three wise men. Mary and Joseph gazed lovingly upon the ceramic child of Jesus in the manager. Christmas in South Dakota began when Mom unpacked the manger from the dusty boxes stored in the basement the other eleven months of the year. It was always a magical time.

Vonnie and I stood in our saddle shoes, uncomfortable in our hated long brown stockings and heavy, durable clothing, transfixed. Mom placed the music box on the lower part of the end table, giving us the opportunity to watch it rotating and wonder. I loved the music box and what it represented. The warmth around us disguised the cold outside. And we loved Mom's Christmases.

Christmas was notoriously joyous. One of the first big events of the season was when Mom and Dad took us to the annual Santa Claus Day at the Legion Hall, where *The Little Rascals* was shown on the large screen. Then Santa arrived amidst the children's squeals. Santa handed out bags of candy, peanuts, and pieces of fruit, usually an orange or apple.

Mom's special touch left no aspect of the holiday untouched, especially the treats. She made Lefsa, Russian teacakes, and fig cookies called wedding cakes, which were

Karren's favorite. She baked Christmas bread, with candied green and red cherries, as well as spritz cookies, and a white melt-in-your-mouth candy called divinity. Hundreds of Mom's famous popcorn balls, made lovingly by her hands, were consumed by little mouths.

She would make lutefisk and oyster stew for Christmas Eve, and that was part of what made that day glorious. Christmas Eve day beginning with a thorough cleaning of everything. First the house. Then, through the sacrament of confession, our souls. On Christmas Eve day, before any celebration of Christ's birth, we were trotted off to confession. In Mom's home, both cleanings were mandatory.

Mom made every holiday special. On May 1, Mom worked tirelessly to make May baskets for us to deliver. She made Halloween, Valentine's Day, July 4th, equally wonderful. And Saint Patrick's Day was a holy day in our home. Birthday celebrations she knocked out of the ballpark. And she was taught this by whom?

In fact, Mom's presence graced so many moments. She sang to us. After she tucked us in after prayers, "Irish Lullaby" rolled off her lips as she set on the edge of our bed, softly singing the song I imagined Grandma Bessie sang to her. It was my favorite. She sang others: "The Baggage Coach Ahead," a song about a young father who holds his crying child while the other passengers impatiently ask, "Where is its mother?" The father replies, "She is dead in the baggage coach ahead."

"The Lonely Little Robin" was another song she sang:

The lonely little robin in a tree by my door
who waits for his mate to return evermore.

So remember, yes, remember that I'm lonely, too,
like the lonely little robin in the tree by my door.

The other song was about two babes who die in the woods. Mom's songs were sad. They sang of her sadness. Her losses. Perhaps her singing was a way to voice the grief too difficult to display. Or perhaps it was a remnant of her Irish ancestry.

There were more things about Mom that were serious than just her songs. When one of our "crimes" (lying, stealing, or bullying a sibling) was exposed, Mom made a huge production of burning the blessed palms from Palm Sunday. As children, we knew this was a big deal, since we were never allowed to touch the blessed palms, but could only look at them and be reminded of something that happened right before Jesus died on the cross and the Easter Bunny came. Mom would then proceed to fingerprint each of us, using the ashes of the blessed palm. Needless to say, the confession occurred from the culprit prior to him or her being printed. Mom was good. She perfected this practice prior to entering the field of law enforcement. Early on, it was in her veins.

"Sister Marsha said..." It was a refrain we often heard, and the tone of Mom's voice implied the moral aptitude of the impressive nun who taught Mom right from wrong in her childhood. Today, I realize Mom was a master of Catholic guilt. In reality, she was forming our consciences. And she was taught by the likes of Sister Marsha, who told her students of the promise she made to her fiancé to become a nun if he died in the war. He did. And she kept that, as well as another, promise; she became a nun and kept a lock of his hair.

Of course, according to Mom, Sister received special dispensation to keep the hair since religious orders steered away from all things temporal. The message from Mom, via Sister Marsha, was usually about commitment and staying with your obligation. Fidelity. No matter what.

Father Flakins, the formidable priest of her childhood she feared but respected. I blamed him for Mom's ability to inspire paralyzing fear when it came to talking with us about sexual feelings and behaviors. Mom's toughness was apparent when telling her daughters that if they ever became pregnant before marriage, the child would be released for adoption. She would follow this statement with, "It would kill me to give up a grandchild; however, no child deserves to be raised by a child." Not one of her daughters became pregnant before marriage. However, she forgot to give the same message to her sons.

We knew Mom meant business. We were raised with Father Falkins Sex Education Course. Sister Marsha, Father Falkins, the strong values and faith from her mother and, at times, her father, served Mom well as she, a stunningly beautiful young woman, was thrown to the world alone and survived with her morals intact.

"Mom, Annetta's head is bleeding. It's split wide open," screamed Vonnie as she ran up the steps from our newly poured concrete basement floor. Vonnie and I had come up with the brilliant idea of making a swing in the basement. The results meant that Inez Hough, our drugstore saint, had to tape me back together. She also gave me candy as she taped me.

Small towns foster an inordinate amount of special, interesting characters. I called them saints. Inez was one. Lucy and Heine Ostwinkle were our ice cream saints (they also owned Heine's Barber Shop). The Ostwinkles served the most seductive, magnificent ice cream in South Dakota. Ole Anderson, the leather saint, was a miracle worker with leather, saving many a pair of shoes. He came from Norway via Minnesota, as had many in our town. Ruth and Walter "Watchy" Lawien owned the hardware store. Today, entering the door of a real hardware store immediately takes me back to Lawien's Hardware Store, which smelled of sawdust and nails. The smell of leather takes me to Ole's little shoe shop.

But no one matched Marge. She was our community saint. Before the publishing of Rachel Carson's *Silent Spring* in 1962, Marge Katus lived the epitome of recycling. Our first meeting was the night Mom and Dad were shivereed. It was a local tradition. In the dark of the night, usually after newlyweds were in bed, the neighbors would make a racket with any noisemaker they could find, including pots and pans. They'd yell and whistle, and after the noise died down, there was celebrating with food and drink.

Of course, in my parents' case, the newlywed couple in question had four young children in tow. We had just arrived in McIntosh. We had parked Dad's small gray camper trailer behind the home of Grandma Erz, Dad's friend John Erz's mother. Our new Dad had been living there before the wedding. Hearing the noise and banging, the four of us huddled in the corner of the trailer, knowing we were going to die. The door to our small trailer flew open and there stood a flaming redhead who saved us four huddled, petrified kids. It was the first of a million times that Marge Katus comforted us.

When I think of the women of McIntosh, Leona Senftner, Irene Erz, June Swanson, Helen Baumburger, Grandma Lenerville, Franklyn Hanson, Lena Olson, Shirley Dillman,

Verna Jacobs, and my mother, LaVerna Kittelson, immediately come to mind. They were—and are—models for living a good life. Among all those fabulous women, Marge Katus stood out. She was a true Renaissance woman. Marge was more than a neighbor; she was a teacher, friend, mentor, and role model. She truly was a second mom to many of us.

I realized long ago her influence in my life. I am a dogged recycler because of Marge. The priorities I place on education, reading, creativity, openness to all, resisting racism, and so much more I got from her. And politics. She was the best and brightest. Marge loved me unconditionally, as did two other maternal figures, Leona Senftner and Shirley Dillman. All that unconditional love: it impacted me immensely.

Chapter 5

"I'm running for Sheriff," Dad announced as he walked through the door. "What's a sheriff?" Vonnie asked. We had no clue. Roy Rogers rushed through my head.

In 1956, George Seiler Sr. and Fred Blow, two prominent Democrats in our very Republican county, asked Dad to run for the office of Corson County sheriff. The closest thing Dad had to law enforcement training was trying to parent four fatherless children and living with Mom, an itinerant "cop" in her own right.

Everyone in our family became a campaign worker. Dad ran for sheriff of Corson County in 1956. Mom was his campaign manager. His children were campaign volunteers, handing out cards with Dad's picture on them and his quotes about his desire to be their sheriff. We went door to door. Car to car.

He won. As he became a public servant, so did his entire family. Thus began the journey of living with a minister who wore a badge. Later, Mom became his deputy. His children, assistant deputies. For the rest of Dad's and Mom's work lives, election night determined our livelihood.

The emergency lights flickered against the sea of wheat and the gravel road. Two touches on the siren. He gave his signature one-finger wave and shouted "Come on, move it." The cows slowly looked up to view their intruder. Chewing quietly on their cuds, they casually moved their large bodies toward the ditch. He got out of the lime green Ford and shouted, "C'mon. Move it. Move it."

Waving his arms, he watched the cows move lazily towards the pasture, where a broken fence had provided the escape. As he opened the door to the car, he muttered half to me, half to himself, "Dan's fence needs repair." He put the car in drive, turned off the flashing police lights, and drove slowly down the gravel road to notify their owner.

We drove down the lane to Dan's place, a longtime farmer and rancher. He greeted Dad. "Hi, Harry. What brings you out?" He leaned against the car.

"Oh, no," I thought and cringed inside. I know what that meant; the lean was a preparation, a preparation for a couple hours of conversation. What Dad called "shooting the bull." The cows were an excuse. Dad loved a good visit with one of his multitude of friends. His constituents. They voted him to the office of Corson County sheriff for thirty-two years. They lovingly called him "The Sheriff." We just called him Dad.

When he assumed his office, he became not only *our* protector, but also the fatherly protector of over 2,473 miles of South Dakota prairie, including the Standing Rock Indian Reservation, along with its people. Harry Kittelson served as Corson County sheriff beginning in November 1956, "retiring" in 1983, and for the next eight years, patrolling the Oahe Dam for Corson County for the US Army Corps of Engineers.

Often referring to himself as a peace officer, not a police officer, he delivered babies and maintained that locking people in handcuffs or in a jail cell only demeaned their humanity. He welcomed thousands of people of every nationality and socioeconomic status to sit at our family table and spent hours counseling his "charges" to use common sense. He was a counselor, physiatrist, human-relations expert, business manager, and CEO. And the only time he ever entered a university was when he moved one of us to college dorms.

He never carried a gun, causing Judge Robert Tschetter, colleague and friend, to reflect that he "would never see Harry live to retire." Instead of using a firearm, Dad believed in the art of persuasion and human compassion. He lived into retirement and beyond. He also influenced other local law enforcement officers with his gentle and effective direction.

One of Dad's responsibilities was to feed the prisoners. In the over thirty years of his public service, I never remember my father actually arresting anyone. I never remember him placing anyone in jail, although he visited with those who were there. The tribal and city police made the arrests. Some of the prisoners came from other jurisdictions. And my father fed them.

Sometimes I went with him. Going with Dad to the old county jail, located across from the courthouse, was like walking into hell. One bare lightbulb hung from the ceiling. It was painted a military dark green and smelled of urine. The one toilet stood in what was called the bullpen. Two smaller cells contained within the larger space had bunks hanging from the wall. They provided a snippet of privacy. A hotplate with two burners was home to two coffee cans the prisoners used to cook food. The hotplate was plugged in to the extended blub with a plug attached.

It was a dim, dark, smelly, and foul environment. The

prisoners lit up when my father entered the door. Dad called it "feeding the birds." He opened the door, flooding the living hell with both sunlight and compassion.

"Hi, Harry," someone would call out, and so the chatter began. Dad sat and visited with what he felt were his people. He loved the people of his county. And they loved him.

Beside the bullpen was a cell painted bright gray. One bunk, toilet, and sink made up what was called the female cell. It was the place where Dad delivered more than one baby. The city or tribal police would place a woman in the cell at night and in the morning, when Dad went to feed the prisoners, there were two: a woman and her newborn baby. Or sometimes a woman would be crying in labor, ready to deliver, and Dad would bring a beautiful new human being to the stench of that Godawful place. One baby was born in the filthy toilet. Every single person placed in that jail was there due to alcohol consumption or abuse, or what today we know to be alcoholism.

Dad became a staunch advocate to eliminate the unsafe, unsanitary, and unwanted hellhole. Fortunately, the federal law worked with him, because a new jail was built with a new office, as well as living quarters for the county sheriff and his family. It was there that I continued to watch my father visit, counsel, and encourage people to change their lives and become productive citizens. Prisoners sat at our kitchen table, in the living room. We even had prisoners babysit the younger siblings. Dad called it sleeping in the jail without the door being locked.

Dad had no formal law enforcement training. Educational process came through the farm, ranch jobs, graduating from Thunder Hawk High School, the CCC (the Civilian Conservation Corps was a public work relief program that

operated from 1933 to 1942 in the United States for unem-
ployed, unmarried men, part of President Franklin Roos-
evelt's New Deal Depression era program), and being a father.

~

Politics became our family lifeblood, because the sheriff's
office was an elected position. Although Dad ran for office,
Mom was the one who loved it. Politics pulsed in Mom's
veins. George McGovern and Hubert Humphrey, John and
Bobby Kennedy: these names echoed in our home as often
as "God" and the "Blessed Mother."

I, too, love politics—in all of its messiness and corrup-
tion, the always-exciting debates. My passion for politics
came directly from Mom. My father ran and won in land-
slides for years in a very Republican state, a very Republican
county, and Mom played a critical role in his wins.

One vote that Dad knew he never received was his
father's, Grandpa's. "Dad always voted straight ticket. One
check: Republican," Dad told me. But Mom and Dad always
voted for the person, not the party. Yet they were also loyal
Democrats. Mom felt strongly about protecting the democratic platforms for the poor. For her, it was the social programs that cemented her commitment, especially the ones
promising to bring people out of the destitution caused by the
Depression. And she believed it was what the church taught.

And she hated war. Mom felt strongly about peace while
standing up to anyone who attempted to stop soldiers from
receiving respect. Having lived through WWII—deeply
impacted by WWI—she loved veterans and was herself a
lifelong American Legion Auxiliary member. The poppy,
adopted by the ALA as its memorial flower, Mom loved as

much as she did roses. She taught us her favorite beloved poem, written a year before her birth.

IN FLANDERS FIELD

In Flanders Field the poppies blow
Between the crosses row on row,
That mark our place; and in the sky
The larks, still bravely singing, fly
Scarce heard amid the guns below.

We are the Dead. Short days ago
We lived, felt dawn, saw sunset glow,
Loved and were loved, and now we lie
In Flanders Field.

Take up our quarrel with the foe:
To you from failing hands we throw
The torch; be yours to hold it high.
If ye break faith with us who die
We shall not sleep, though poppies grow
In Flanders Field.
    —Lt. Col. John McCrae

She was progressive in her thought. Strongly opposed to abortion, she also felt strongly about it not being a political platform and opposed politicians who used the issues to be elected. She grew up knowing about a local woman who helped out girls in bad situations. She also knew of the coat hanger and the desperation, often both the baby and woman dying.

In fact, she once told me that no one protected young women who had been taken advantage of or impregnated by their own relatives. Today we call it rape and incest. Back then, there were only "situations." Mom knew of a significant number of these "situations" taken care of in back alleys. She also knew of the women in the area who provided those services; Mom told me of her empathy for the young women and the person who helped them. "What they must have suffered," was Mom's response. Mom didn't judge, and she provided homes for abandoned and neglected children. It was Catholic social teaching at its best.

The Kennedys, feeding programs, and civil rights were close to her heart, yet Mom was a dichotomy when it came to racial issues. Her behavior, often a contradiction, confused me more than once. She provided homes, care, and encouragement to Native American children. It came natural to her to give supportive space to the Native American women to make traditional star quilts. But all that changed when it came to African Americans.

Not until I was older did I understand her struggle and fear of African Americans. Her brother Jim, stabbed and left for dead, pushed Mom to a dark place when she encountered an African American. The man who stabbed Uncle Jim happened to be an African American. This incident hurt my mom deeply, and she could not forgive. She saw it as hurting her brothers, and the struggle in her heart was intolerable. She took the stabbing personally and couldn't look past the skin color of the person responsible. I saw it differently, very differently. Alcohol played a role the night of the stabbing, for both the perpetrator and victim.

When it came to childrearing, Dad practiced a distinctive psychology.

"Time to do dishes," Dad said one day without fanfare.

Mom and Wally were attending a family funeral in Iowa, and Dad was left in charge of us three grade-school girls. Karren, without hesitation, began picking up the dishes. Vonnie and I, thinking we were getting away with the responsibility of doing dishes, carefully moved to the living room where we began to play. Much to our delight, Dad and Karren completed the task. For Vonnie and me, doing dishes was right up there with the death penalty for the kids in the Kittelson home: we hated it. Our smug attitude changed, though, when Dad sat a chair in the middle of the dining room floor facing the buffet.

He invited Vonnie and me to sit on the chairs on the side of the buffet. We did so happily, thinking it was a game. But is wasn't. Our smugness fell to the floor when Dad invited Karren to sit in the chair facing us.

He thanked her, saying, "Without being asked, you helped with the dishes. For that you receive this." Our mouths fell open when Dad handed her a bag filled with candy-covered peanuts.

To this day, I hate candy-covered peanuts.

Dad's ability to use reverse psychology became legendary. He never criticized. He never doled out put-downs. He gave us life lessons. His perspective was: when you participate in life and live responsibly without hesitation, then life can produce sweet things like candy. We learned this through his actions. He never even needed to use words.

Structure permeated family life in our household. We had mandatory family meals. Everyone's place at the table was secure: meals were at noon and six o'clock. Prayer began the meal, followed by discussion of the day's events. Mom and Dad were always there, invited guests were a common occurrence. And we children knew what was expected of us: to listen.

Mom determined the menu, cooked with our assistance, and we were to eat without whining. Whining did not happen in our house. "You will eat what is on the table," Mom and Dad said. There was no need to say it twice. Mom and Dad, Depression-era survivors, knew hunger. No one questioned their wisdom. We ate what was placed in front of us. And we did so until our plate was clean. There was no waste. And my father always said, "There is to be no grazing." According to Dad, that's what families did that never sit down at a table and shared a meal. In other words, meals were sacred at our home. It was the time for family to come together. And we did.

Dad's wisdom stretched far beyond the walls of our home. He knew who owned what piece of land along miles of rolling prairie; he knew the previous owner and whether the land had been handed down through the generations. If a farmer were in a field when Dad passed by in his sheriff's car, he waited until the farmer reached the end of the row, then they'd sit there for hours, visiting.

As he traversed the area at night when there wasn't a soul in sight, moving from farm to town on the gravel roads, Dad would pull any car, pickup, or farm truck that popped up over the horizon aside for a visit. He'd open the door of his patrol car, the farmer would get out of his often-rusted, spent truck, and they'd visit, sometimes for hours.

I often rode with Dad, and so I sat and listened for hours, too. I learned many of life's lessons listening to those conversations. I heard hundreds of snippets, like "That damn fool built his house right by the water. The first time a flood happens he will have water up to his ass and wonder why" and "Your neighbor is spreading manure. Wise man. It is the smell of money." I didn't understand the meaning of some phrases until adulthood, but I absorbed it all nevertheless.

Dad's involvement in the community as a sheriff affected life at home, too. Mom's famous Christmas celebrations changed slightly when our family entered law enforcement, for example. I remember one in particular.

"George is drunk. He's beating Anna and the children are terrified," Mom said, turning from the phone one Christmas Eve. This became one of our Christmas Eve rituals: Dad receiving domestic violence calls because someone had consumed too much alcohol. The drinking caused hell in many homes and affected the children especially.

That particular Christmas Eve, Dad, with Mom's warning to be careful, got behind the wheel of his green sheriff patrol car and drove to George and Anna's home, bringing Anna and the seven children to our home for respite. It would give George time to sleep it off. Filled with sadness and fear, the weary little family was greeted with Mom's warmth.

Vividly remembering these moments, I sponsored one of the daughters years later in Al-Anon, becoming godmother to her and three of their children. Later, I spoke at the funeral of one of the godchildren who had been killed in an alcohol-related accident.

This was not the only family Mom and Dad brought to our home on a Christmas Eve. Over the years, there were countless. Alcoholism did not take a vacation on Christmas Eve. Offering food, warmth, shelter, and gifts, Mom and Dad tried to lessen the pain it caused.

Mom fed the entire county in some way during the Christmas season. The school administration, teachers, and staff; county workers; and law enforcement officers all had their own separate gatherings each year. And on Christmas Day, Mom invited anyone in the community who was alone to our home. Mom even gave gifts to the prisoners, the people Dad described as just "sleeping in our jail." Some were there because of crimes they had committed; others just needed a place to sleep. No matter. Mom believed everyone deserved "a little gift on Christmas."

The tiny newborn baby lying in the hospital's nursery had a badge on its chest. "Deputy Sheriff," it read. Dad's first biological son was born on June 8, 1957. Joseph Clarence Kittelson. Dad was thrilled. The rest of us were insane with joy, lavishing attention on Joey, as we called him, and surrounding him with love.

"Mom and little Joey are coming home," Dad told us already-excited siblings a few days after his birth. When they arrived, however, Mom never left the bed. Irene Erz and the other women in McIntosh cooked meals, waited on Mom, and took care of baby Joey. Mary Ann Trager, a local nurse, carried bedpans of blood from Mom's bed to the bathroom. Vonnie and I were scared.

"What's that?" Vonnie asked me.

"It must be from Mom's leg," was my brilliant, naïve reply. We had no knowledge of where babies came from or what could happen to a woman after the birth of a child.

The next morning Dad, John Erz, and two more men whose names I cannot remember carried Mom out of the house, returning her to the hospital. Mary Ann carried Joey; he went to the hospital with Mom. The rest of us had no idea what was happening. Requests for blood went out across the area.

"Harry, she's gone," Doctor Torklison said to Dad as Father O'Rourke, our parish priest, provided the last rites. Doc pronounced her dead. Mother proved him wrong.

"I could hear them talking about me," Mom later said.

Dr. Torklison, a fervent Catholic, told Dad that Mom's recovery was a miracle. "Harry, I had nothing to do with it. As far as I was concerned, LaVerna was gone. Someone greater provided the miracle."

Joe lived with the knowledge his birth almost caused mother's death. Perhaps that's why he was unabated in his devotion to Mom as he grew to adulthood. Until his life took a sudden course away from her, Joe showed mother total unselfishness.

When he returned as an infant with Mom from the hospital, we older sisters took care of him, protected him. We knew early on that there was something special about Joe. He had unique qualities. Only later did we understand why.

When Dad married us, our parents asked Wally if he wanted us to be adopted by Dad. "No, I want to keep my dad's name," he responded. At the time, I didn't like Wally's response. And as time passed, I liked it even less. After Mom's near-death experience, I often wondered, "If Mom died, what would have happened, since Dad has never legally adopted us?" It was a fear I held deep in my heart.

"Call Harry and LaVerna" was a common phrase in our county. For any accident, Dad was called. Mom, from home, with the phone and police radio, contacted the hospital, the doctor, sometimes the minister, more likely the parish priest. When Dad called Mom on the police radio for "Cecil," it meant the victim was dead. Cecil was our country corner. The call to Cecil was always followed by a call to the mortician.

As a law enforcement family, our life took on a unique hue. However, since a rather untraditional couple headed our household, out-of-the-ordinary experiences occurred just about daily. One memory is etched in my mind, and it shows what can happen when people see one another with different eyes.

The night the Iranians came to dinner started as a mundane family night. Mom was preparing the nightly meal. We kids were doing our nightly duties. It was routine. All was calm. Then Mom received a phone call. It was Dad calling from his office; he was bringing a couple of Iranian fellows home to spend the night.

Mom turned pale as she sat the phone down in its base. An expression of complete shock spread across her face. "Your dad is bringing two men home from Iran who wanted to sleep in the jail for the night. He said they were sleeping here and we would feed them a good home-cooked meal."

"What's Iran?" I asked while I completed my nightly chores. It was 1955. Dwight Eisenhower lived in the White House on Pennsylvania Avenue. We had no idea what or where Iran was.

I, the dutiful child, was setting the table. It was my turn. "Your turn" involved setting the table, washing the dishes, and helping Mom in the kitchen. I resumed my task, unmoved. Iranians? Then I had a brilliant thought. "Maybe they ran. I-ran." Although the idea was funny, even I concluded that it couldn't be right. Then I thought, "Dad is always bringing someone home. Mom probably has the name wrong."

Mom pressed red lipstick on her lips, combed her rich, auburn hair, smoothed her cotton dress, and turned to each of us, combing our blond locks. Then the guests arrived. Dad introduced Mom first to the two young men—very polite— with dark hair, beautiful black eyes, and gentle smiles. Then he introduced them to the five of us children (by this time, our little sister, Mary, had joined us).

We learned that they were on their way on a motorcy- cle to Washington, DC, to present a token of peace, a hand- made Iranian rug created by the Iranian people, to President Dwight Eisenhower. In our very Democratic home, we wel- comed not only the strangers, but also their message and the respect they were showing our president, a Republican, a president whom every member of our family respected.

We invited town folks in that evening, so our interest- ing strangers could share their story of travel across the United States, as well as details about their culture, land, and people. It was a fascinating night, anything but routine. Sometime later, Mom and Dad received a letter from Issa and Abdullah Ommidvar, thanking them for their hospital- ity. It read:

> Dear Mr. and Mrs. Kittelson,
>
> There is a Persian word "Kismet" (Destiny or fate) which is eventually has come into English literature and really kind kismet brought us about you, the most won- derful family.

We naturally are fortunate meeting many people along the way. BUT only a few of them left some unforgetful memories, we have been constantly remembering you and utterly proud of having met and known you.

After we left you in that miserable condition we could only drive about 250 miles. I continue to feel badly. Temperature went high, fewer, oh I was burning, finally took two days. Now we are in Lansing as a jumping off place to the Hudson Bay is where we are going to spend the winter.

Hope, this letter will find you under the best of every thing and if the phenomenon of New Invention be a reason to promote the world peace, we shall come over the next time to meet you by satellite.

Please extend our regards to the friends. We shall be glad hearing you. Sincerely yours, Issa and Abdullah Ommidvar Iranian Explorers

Mom and Dad promoted world peace in a little home in McIntosh, South Dakota, just by feeding and sheltering two men of an unknown culture. In that time and place, it didn't matter these visitors' beliefs, their dialect, or the US president's political party. Harry and LaVerna fed, sheltered, and loved the strangers riding a motorcycle.

In stark contrast to the peace and serenity in our home and community, a dark truth lurked in the homes and families of many in our community. Across the country, even. And no one talked about it.

Alcohol was affecting almost every home in my hometown. Alcohol establishments outnumbered most other businesses. A man in our community used to claim, "You can buy all the booze you want after six o'clock, but nary a quart of milk." In the early days of our town, stories were told of town drunkenness and raucous behavior. Some things never changed.

A significant number of my childhood friends' fathers drank alcohol. I later discovered that a significant number of them not only drank, but also suffered from the disease of alcoholism.

Coming to school in the third grade, a classmate told my best friend he saw her father with a "squaw going in to the motel." I was horrified. I wanted to protect my friend. It was normal for my friend's father to be seen with a woman other than his wife. But I didn't think my friend really knew.

"Squawing" was a term bigoted white people used when a white man had sex with a Native American woman, often because she needed alcohol and he wanted sex. Perhaps she was even suffering from the disease herself; for a cheap drink, he took favors. While some people tended to look the other way, the tongues of others wagged in mock satisfaction at their knowledge; they were jubilant in their gossiping.

To be honest, this use and abuse of Indian women was just one kind of egregious behavior toward the Native Americans who lived on the reservation near our home. Often grocery store owners would hike the price of groceries when the Native American people received their monthly allotment checks and did their monthly shopping. Native American people were treated differently. What I knew of it, I hated.

Another childhood friend's father worked hard six days a week, leaving work to spend the rest of the night at the local American Legion. Just as some took the same pews in church week after week, some sat on the same bar stool every night; the regulars called the bar stool by that person's name. This man sat on the same stool every night. He was a veteran of WWII. Many of the regulars at the legion were. Nightly or weekly bar visits were normal for many families. I never saw this friend's father attend anything she did in school. It made me sad for her.

It was as if most of my friends and I lived on opposite but parallel tracks. I grew up in a home where my parents never missed a church or school function, program, recital, ball game, or anything with which we were involved. Some of my friends' parents were never present. We always knew when we looked out in the bleachers that we'd catch a glimpse of Mom and Dad.

The parish priest came often to eat in our home and to visit; we held a respectful but realistic view of him, and he was a normal part of our lives. We didn't put him on a pedestal. For us, priests provided solace, friendship, and a steady presence in our family. Our family provided the same in return. Priests were comfortable with us.

In later years, working as a diocesan director with clergy sexual abuse, I reflected on the significance of what occurred in my childhood home. As a child, one of my favorite parish priests, Father O'Rourke, a funny man with an Irish brogue, provided me with an early insight into the lonely world of a country priest.

When I was a first grader, Mom told me, "If the snow storm becomes worse and school closes early, go to Father's house." Father's house, the rectory of our parish, was located next to our public grade school. I was to wait there until Mom or Dad could come to pick me up. I prayed for the storm.

The snow storm came. I went to Father's house. As a first

grader, I loved visiting with Father O'Rourke. I sat across from him trying not to look at the Snickers bar in the crystal dish next to the over-stuffed chair. I liked listening to him, to the wonderful, lilting Irish way he spoke. And his words were peppered with his Irish wit, a slight hint of spit always at the corner of his mouth, especially when he became excited. I loved Father O'Rourke.

On that snowy afternoon, a sudden knock on the door startled us both. My very Lutheran and, as was common in those days, anti-Catholic grandfather, stood in the doorway. "I came to pick her up," was Grandpa's command. He spoke no other words to the priest. Father attempted conversation, but to no avail. For the first and only time in my memory, Grandpa took my small-gloved hand in his as we went out into the windy, cold, snowy day. I looked back. Father stood in the door, waving.

In my innocence, something of an understanding came over me at that moment, which was confirmed later that night by Mom. I asked, "Why does Father have to live in that big house all alone?"

Mom replied, "It is the life he chose so he could teach us about God."

I didn't like the answer. The loneliness and emptiness I saw at the door of the rectory that day remained etched in my mind. I also never forgot that Father forgot to give me a Snickers bar.

It is hard today to imagine the leap of faith men had to take to pursue the priestly vocation in the days prior to the reform ushered in by Pope John XXIII in the 1950s and '60s. More than once, a priest passed out at the altar. Not from alcohol, although a fair amount suffered—and suffer—from the disease, but from hours of fasting, wearing heavy vestments, and the mental and physical exhaustion.

My first real religious rebellion came during Mass and it involved Mike Brick, a tall, distinguished, white-haired bachelor who worked for a local alcoholic farmer. Mike, one of the many bachelors my parents lovingly reached out to over the years, had the habit of holding out candy to me during Mass. I became proficient in crawling under the pew, until one day Dad caught me reaching for the glorious sweetness. I never did find out if Dad talked to Mike or, to protect my life, Mike ceased and desisted.

Another rebellious experience happened when I attended a Father Peyton Family Rosary Rally in the Black Hills. I hated it. His message is imbedded in my brain: "The family that prays together, stays together." While the message was good, it was one of the most physically miserable days of my life. The weather was cold, windy. Mom felt it necessary that we wear dresses to such an important event; as a result, I was freezing. It was torture. Mom liked suffering for the faith, felt it was necessary, in fact. In my young mind, I thought that Father Peyton must, too. My rebellion. I had a bad thought about Father Peyton and Mom. Maybe it was more than one bad thought. It was so bad I ended up going to confession over it. Catholic scrupulosity begins early and stays late, even at rosary crusades.

In the fourth grade, my sister Vonnie and I began to clean the rectory, Father's house. By this time, a temporary priest, Father Szealy, had replaced Father O'Rourke. Father Szealy was a gentle giant of a man. Weekly, we cleaned the bedrooms, front room, dining room, kitchen, and bathrooms, which we believed were for the parishioners, not

Father. In our brilliant innocence, Vonnie and I concluded that no priest could possible participate in any bodily functions, being so filthy.

Our theory changed when, as a dinner guest, Father used our bathroom. Unaware, I walked in the unlocked bathroom and found Father, back turned to me, standing at the lavatory. It was a major life event. "He's like us. He's human!" screamed in my head. I ran and told Vonnie. She was pensive about the news and didn't seem to really grasp its significance.

Every Saturday morning we filled the rectory with pungent, sweet smells as we scrubbed, vacuumed, and polished the furniture. Father Szealy suffered untold misery from ulcers. He served us ice cream and crisp vanilla finger cookies. "It's the only thing I can eat," he said. Upon completion of our tasks, Father taught us how to play marbles using a string to form a circle on the rug. We'd also dress in his cassocks, collar, and coat. Vonnie and I loved to play church. When we did it at home, we used our homemade swing for the communion rail and Necco candy for the host. It really was about the candy, not prayer.

Mom held out eternal hope that one of her children would enter either the priesthood or religious life, giving nun dolls to Vonnie and me one year for Christmas. The doll lived in a Benedictine habit. In the era of my childhood, most young Catholics considered priesthood or religious life. It happened for me in fourth grade. I wanted to be like Saint Theresa of the Little Flower. It was a fleeting moment, however. After all, I loved boys, and the only boy Saint Theresa seemed to like was her dad, so I dismissed the thought.

But I nevertheless had a rather religious frame of mind, and this made dressing in Father Szealy's priestly garb entirely natural. Father laughed at our antics. Vonnie and I snapped pictures of the three of us dressed in collars. So as third and fourth graders, Vonnie and I were the first female priests. It was never a question for Father Szealy. We loved our Saturday forays at Father's and never took pay. Mom told us we were helping God when we helped Father. So our pay was hanging out with Father.

Sometimes I think he enjoyed the company as much as we enjoyed the freedom and attention. He kept a tin on the top of the buffet, placing money in it every week after we cleaned, later giving it to Mom for us to go to camp.

Father Szealy loved to make funny faces. He did it with all the children of the parish. He was beloved by each and every person. I loved Father Szealy; he was one of the most remarkable men of my life.

Significant impressions imprint in the mind of a child, and several impressions remain with me about the priests coming through our little parish. Some were able to offer true pastoral care; some were not so gifted. I recall the time a boy was chewing gum during Mass, blowing bubbles. The priest who followed Father Szealy wore the same Roman collar, although he did not possess the same temperament. He, impatient and intolerant, told the boy sternly, from the lectern, to bring his gum and place it on the communion rail.

In those days, we knelt at the rail to receive Communion. As I knelt to receive it that Sunday, perched on the railing was that wad of gum. The boy, who without the support of parents had attended Mass alone, didn't retrieve the gum. I never again saw the boy at Mass. Nor did I hear of him attending any other church in our small community. Years later, I learned his parents died of alcoholism.

During mandatory Holy Week confession, I nervously

confessed my usual sins and responded to our then current priest with a "Yeah, Father." It did not sit well with him. What followed was a curt scolding. He said, "You are to say 'Yes, Father.'" The terror I felt was only tempered by the fact I was behind a screen. Yet only a skimpy curtain separated me from the body of the church. The place was packed. I knew every soul in the church that day, and I knew they heard Father let me have it.

As I came from the confessional to pray my penance, I was filled with shame and humiliation. It was with humiliation that some pastors, as well as come religious women and educators, delivered the message. It worked for me. These experiences terrified me. To this day, I thank Pope John XXIII for opening up the window to let the spirit in. It was called Vatican II. Although humiliating messages still come from the mouths of some priests, it was more common pre-Vatican II. Humiliation does not work on the soul of anyone, especially children.

Through the example of my parents and other faith-filled Catholics, including Irene Erz, my faith as a child remained innocent, pure. Two people who ministered with a badge raised me. My parents cared for homeless, abandoned, and neglected children. Today, we call it foster care; our parents called it human care. They emulated what the gospel teaches.

In many areas, Mom and Dad possessed similar philosophies. Today, I marvel at the prophetic nature of some of those philosophies.

Each had a natural compassion and affinity for others. Dad's one-finger wave rose as he passed every car. He knew them. If he didn't, he found out by stopping and visiting. Mom would often say, as we passed a vacated farm, abandoned long ago and sitting among the stubble fields, the sound of a wind mill humming and miles of bellowing prairie grass surrounding it, "If those walls could talk, the stories they would tell," referring to the joy and pain that must have been felt there. She taught us to stop and pick the wild flowers harbored in the fields beside those vacant farms.

"It's the ruination of the family," Dad responded when Wally came home and announced he was playing basketball games twice a week. "Two nights a week!" Dad exclaimed. "The family will be out of the home two nights a week? Then it will be three, and pretty soon, families will never see each other." They were prophetic words.

Chapter 6

"You make me sick," Mom said through clenched teeth. The weapon came out: Mom's long, well-kept fingernails. I jumped as they pinched and pierced my skin. It was another one of those moments when I literally did not know what I had done wrong. Like many mothers and daughters, Mom and I had a complicated relationship. The first years of life, until I was twenty-seven years old, I was consumed with trying to get Mom's approval. I received bits and pieces of it toward the end.

My sister Karren said it was because we were so much alike. She was the family truth bearer. Mom and I *were* alike, although there were stark differences. I have many of Mom's strengths, as well as similar weaknesses. I often tell people, "Mom loved me. But I often wondered whether she liked me."

I knew from childhood there was something about me that disgusted her. It was obvious. I spent my life attempting to understand what it was. She was dismissive of me. I never felt unconditional love, only the strength of her critical look. The clenched teeth.

One particularly severe episode occurred in the third grade. I was reading a book in my bedroom titled *The Pink Maple House*. My best friend, Peggy, had moved, and I was devasted. The book was about a girl whose best friend had moved. I was crying, relating my own loss to the girl in *The Pink Maple House*, when the door opened and Mom, with clenched teeth and obvious anger flowing through her, grabbed the book from my hands and began to beat me with it.

I kept telling her, "It's a library book. It's is not mine. It is a library book." Her only words, interspersed with her strikes, were, "I will pay for the book." I thought that strange, even as I was attempting to avoid the blows of *The Pink Maple House*. What had motivated such an outburst? She never gave a reason.

In those days, I always questioned myself. "I must have done something wrong," I would think to myself. "She is so loving to others; what's wrong with me?" Eventually realizing I had not done anything wrong, I later dismissed such an occurrence as Mom having a bad day. But when it came to our relationship, bad days were common.

Despite the comforts and security established by my parents, I never truly felt safe at home, only at church, or sleeping between my two sisters. Most times, my mother was indifferent to my feelings. Other times, she was condemning or contemptuous, saying things like, "You wear your feelings on your sleeve."

Like most children, I just wanted to be loved and accepted. The birthright of every human being is to know security, stability, nurturance, love, and affirmation. It is the responsibility of parents to provide these things. In my relationship with Mom, I missed receiving several of these. Because of this, I internalized my own emotions. It was only later, in recovery, that I became fully aware of the extent.

I found the only way to receive a modicum of Mom's approval was to clean. So I became the best cleaner in the family. Yet, in adolescence, I found the cleaning often returned to bite me. Mom would often say, "I can't find anything. Annetta was cleaning." I worked extra hard at everything thing I did, telling myself, "Maybe Mom will be happy with me, proud of me." The lack of Mom's acceptance and approval also caused me to be voted "most responsible" my senior year of high school.

Mom didn't know it, but internalizing my feelings at an early age also helped me develop a strong intuition that served me well even into adulthood, both personally and professionally. Father Francis, one of our parish priests, once told me, "Your intuition is only the second highest intuitive I have ever known. The first being Mother Romaine." She was a Benedictine nun I came to know and love in my high school years.

I shared the rejection by my mother with no one, but others in the family seemed to pick up on something. Vonnie attempted to deflect some of Mom's feelings toward me. She was unsuccessful. "For some reason, your Mom was different with you than the others. I loved your Mom, but disagreed in the way she treated you," two of my aunts shared in my adulthood. Their words confirmed what I already knew.

I lived by the fourth commandment: honor your father and mother. This meant having respect for and fidelity to your parents no matter what. It was seared upon my soul. I never knew that honoring did not mean having to agree with them. I didn't know that honoring could mean, God forbid, disagreeing with them. I feared Mom more than God. Yet, I loved her with all my heart.

That question—"She is so good to everyone else, what is wrong with me?"—rose time and time again in my heart during my childhood and adolescence. The question plagued me. Later, I found the answer, but until then, the pain of liv-

ing with the question was searing. In retrospect, this difficult relationship with my mother bore some positive fruit:
my internalizing of my emotions gave rise to the practice of
prayer, a love for my Catholic roots, and empathy, especially
to those people, including alcoholics, suffering sadness, pain,
or rejection. I gained an understanding of their pain through
my own feelings of being disinherited and lonely.

Experiencing the intersection and interconnection between
Catholicism and alcoholism for me began early. I remember when I was in grade school, sitting on the concrete step
outside our house, pleading with Leo, one of the many in
our town who drank too much, to stop drinking. I told him,
"If you stopped drinking, Leo, your mom and dad will stop
being angry at you." In my naiveté, I hadn't realized that his
parents also drank.

The disease of addiction had visited Leo's house long
before my visits with him. Also Catholic, they never missed
Sunday Mass, although they drank every Saturday. I have no
idea if my urgings ever changed Leo's own drinking habits.
To this day, the smell of him is imbedded in my memory.

In the town in which I grew to adulthood, years later
while doing research, I counted the homes that I knew had
been impacted by alcoholism or abusive drinking. It was
approximately 80 percent. The cemeteries in our area are
dotted with people who died prematurely due to alcohol-
related accidents or livers, hearts, and stomachs eaten away
by alcohol. And sad to say, our community was not abnormal.

A culture of drinking persists then and does so today. So
did abject poverty. Today it is the ninth poorest county in

the nation. Although the two do not combine to create the disease, they often are connected and so, too, is culture and sometimes religion.

At Sunday Mass, prior to the new norms set by the Second Vatican Council, the reception of Communion involved the Host, the bread, exclusively; there was no passing of the cup. So detecting the smell of wine on people was relatively easy on Sunday mornings, and it was common. So, too, were the vacant looks on a significant number of family members who had survived the night before.

Chapter 7

"Two points down. Five seconds."

Burying my head in my lap. I couldn't look. Then there was the rip of the buzzer. I looked up as the ball went up and floated through the hoop. The tallest man in McIntosh leaped over my head, his legs barely missing me. The gym exploded. We were going to the state tournament. The little town on the prairie was going to state. It was a first in the history of our school. And my brother was on the first five; so, too, were Dennis, my future brother-in-law, and Homer.

During the fall of 1961, my brother was still in love with his first love, she a Lutheran, he Catholic. "A Catholic will not date my daughter," her mother told a friend. His heart never healed, even though he lost himself in football, basketball, and his classmates. And other girls.

Then in the spring of 1962, Wally was about to graduate after a successful high-school athletic career: first five-state basketball team, first string of the football team, track star, and homecoming king. Our big brother was about to graduate and attend the FBI Academy in Washington, DC. He would be the first in our family to leave the confines of home.

That spring, we siblings all dressed in our 'A' Band uniforms. It was the first and only time the four of us performed together. Wally and Karren played the drums. Vonnie, the flute. I played the clarinet. The piano that Dad had bought paid off for his four children. We stood there together. It had been a long journey from my first blowing a bubble-gum bubble, to burning my hand catching the baseball with Wally to playing in the spring concert with my siblings. It was the last time the four of us were together. Little did any of us know that the most painful part of our journeys were just beginning.

In 1963, our family bought the only remaining hotel in McIntosh. Built in 1911 and first called the Hotel Ecker then Hotel Carson, we named it the Dakota Hotel. We bought it from Alma Irwin and began a badly needed remodel. Our family moved in, along with hundreds of others over the years. We rented rooms by the night, week, or month. The price was $2.50 plus tax a night. You could buy a shower at $.50 with a towel.

Karren, Vonnie, and I, were, as Mom jokingly called us, her "chamber maids." We made the beds, cleaned the rooms, and fed the boarders. The hotel provided rest and food for many sojourners. We were often filled. Feeding the hungry, sheltering the homeless, and giving hope to those in despair, the Dakota Hotel provided the space for Mom and Dad to continue their mission. A significant number of people who had been abandoned without help or who were living with special needs, including mental health issues and addiction, filled many of the rooms.

Winter blizzards, common in our county, often paralyzed the entire area. Blizzards brought stranded human beings to the hotel. On such nights, the hotel burst at the seams, all available beds taken. The spillover slept in the hotel lobby. We hosted anyone needing a warm place. Mom would make large pots of soup to feed the masses. We watched, and helped, our badge-wearing parents ministered to the people.

One of the people who came to live with us at the hotel was Homer White Buffalo. "Homer has nowhere to live. LaVerna, do you think he could stay in a room at the hotel?" asked Glenn Shevlin, the coach who also was our superintendent and who had a heart for his "boys." Mom's rejection of Homer had long been forgotten, and the friendship between Wally and Homer was solid. Mom said, "Absolutely." Homer moved in. He became a son. Mom never again took notice of the color of his skin, unless her second daughter was standing beside him. And for Mom, that never changed.

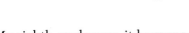

My eighth-grade year, it happened. I fell in love for the first time. He was a junior in high school, entering his senior year. The relationship lasted, although we never married. Homer J. White Buffalo and I stayed together in our heart our entire lives. He told me, when proclaiming his love, "I never want anyone to call you a nigger lover." It did not matter to me. I knew the kind, gentle, loving heart that rested in this man with beautiful black skin. He taught me about racism without saying a thing. The Trail of Tears, the KKK, the Mississippi murders of Michael Schwerner and James Chaney: they were real and we knew it.

A prominent woman once said to me through a sneering laugh, "Black babies. That is what you will have." I had thought well of her until she learned of my relationship with Homer. She did not realize the beauty of black, nor the beauty of all God's multiple colors.

Homer taught me that you can be dealt a horrible hand in life and not only survive, but thrive. Humor was one of his best defenses. His mother, who was Native American, and had been impregnated by an African American man, who, Homer once told me, had literally jumped off the train. After a short time in the area, the man left, and Homer never knew him, at least not until his young adulthood when, by coincidence, he found him .

Homer drifted as a child. Never speaking English until grade school, he received care from his aged grandmother, who gave him what love she could. His mother, a good, kind woman with good, kind sisters, struggled with alcoholism until recovering years later.

As a child, Homer was considered different because of the color of his skin, even in his own culture. Most white people, including my mother, and perhaps most Native Americans saw the color of his skin, not the content of his character, until they allowed themselves to see—really see— the person I saw the first time I laid eyes on him.

Racism destroyed the possibility of us consecrating our love in either a sacramental or legal commitment. But it never destroyed our love. We both had other relationships and fell in love with others, but one thing remained: our devotion to that love. We always showed up for each other. Always. Right to the end.

He had an exquisite voice and often sang two songs to me: "Roses Are Red" by Bobby Vinton and "Blue Angel" by Roy Orbinson. He often wrote beautiful letters, beginning them with, "I thought of you today, as I do every day." Shortly before his death, he told me again, "I love you. I always have." At the end, letting him go was agony.

After graduating from high school, he was drawn to law enforcement, a result of Mom and Dad's influence. He became one of the most respected law enforcement investigators in the Midwest.

Chapter 8

A new breeze was blowing in the Catholic Church. Vatican II. It began on October 11, 1962. The Second Vatican Council convened to address relations between the Roman Catholic Church and the modern world. It was the twenty-first Ecumenical Council of the Catholic Church and the second one to be held at St. Peter's Basilica in the Vatican. How little did I realize the importance of the event held thousands of miles away in Rome, Italy. How little did I understand the influence of Pope John XXIII on an eighth grader in South Dakota.

Less than a year later, I chose to enter a Catholic all-girls boarding school. The decision was due partly to my relationship with Homer; he was leaving to attend college in Huron. The other was the encouragement of my parents; they wanted for each of their children to attend at least one year of Catholic school.

The smell of evergreens filled the air as Mom, Dad, and I drove up the lane to the school. Spruce jetted from the soil, the exquisite beauty of the Black Hills of South Dakota serving as a backdrop. The year was 1963. The place was Saint Martin's Academy in Rapid City, South Dakota. I was fourteen years old.

I met and befriended six special girls that fall: Mary, Ann, Suzan, Yvonne, Fran, and Maura. We all became joined at the hips. And we were filled with things the nuns were not ready to endure.

As we began high school, the culture was emerging from of the innocence of the 1950s and early '60s. But for us girls, life was still full of purity. We had no idea what we were about to face. And then we listened to the music and words of Bob Dylan's "The Times They Are A-Changin.'"

He challenged us, so did the words and ideas of many others. Life as we knew it was changing. The murder of JFK, and later MLK, Jr., and RFK, the Vietnam War, and, of course, the fight for civil rights. These events began to influence everything I did and thought. They encircled the girls of Saint Martin's.

I think of myself as a child of the '60s, but lacking some of the drama. Although I tried cigarettes in the sixth grade with my friend Janet, I hated the taste. I never smoked a joint. Once I tried to drink a beer while attending a Glen Yarbrough concert. Even that didn't pan out; my friends and I became stuck in the mud, and ended up handing over the beer to be consumed by others.

In a way, I was what today is called a nerd. However, I lacked the seriousness of those who really valued traditional education. But rebellion? Now that interested me. I was fascinated by those who actually did it, intrigued by their strength of conviction. Some of what was happening was incongruent with my static surroundings. I felt restless.

While my relationship with Homer was part of that restlessness, it was bigger than that, too. Robert Kennedy said,

Few . . . are willing to brave the disapproval of their fellows, the censure of their colleagues, the wrath of their society. Moral courage is a rarer commodity than bravery in battle or great intelligence. Yet it is the one essential, vital quality for those who seek to change a world which yields most painfully to change.

These words framed my feelings. Strangely, the brokenness in the world began to bring a feeling of liberation to me. In the midst of all this were the Catholic nuns who attempted to teach us, a rare, exceptionally disciplined group of women.

"Jesus, Mary, and Joseph, pray for us." Mention of J. M. J. was prominent at the top of our school papers. I liked that. It served as a reminder. A simple prayer. This was one reason I loved Saint Martin's Academy. And there were other reasons: the high-gloss waxed floors, the spotless dorms, the chapel built with native stone in the form of praying hands, the lines of meticulous desks welcoming an array of young girls from all over the United States. Life was simple—innocent in many ways—and the Benedictines helped keep it that way.

Saint Martin's was built by a group of women. They were trailblazers who built schools, hospitals, universities. They belonged to the Order of Saint Benedict and made up religious communities of men and women who live the mission of Saint Benedict: "Let all Be Received as Christ." Saint Martin's was an example of their mission.

The academy's roots reach back to 1889, to five sisters

from the Benedictine convent of St. Nicholas of Flue in Melchtal, Switzerland. These women of extraordinary faith and tenacity began St. Martin Monastery in Sturgis, South Dakota. The frontier town offered few amenities to Mother Angela Arnet and her companions, and an abandoned tavern served as their first home. Undaunted, within ten days of their arrival, the sisters began a summer school. This was the beginning of St. Martin's Academy.

By 1916, it had developed into a four-year high school. In 1962, the community built a monastery and academy complex in Rapid City, South Dakota, and moved from their original site in Sturgis. It was there, in the new school, where my six new friends and I entered in the fall of 1963.

The impact of the Benedictines on my life is incalculable, beginning with my early childhood and my piano teacher. Each nun of Saint Martin's Academy was rare and unique. They all had brilliant minds, but some were patient, others not. One of my favorites, Sister Marmion, had an especially brilliant scientific mind and a stern presence—until you brought up an interest in science.

Science was not my strong suit. Luckily, my intuition helped me. Not long into the first term, I was failing Sister Marmion's class—fast. I knew that if I wanted to pass and keep my parents happy, I needed to take drastic measures. So I came up with an idea: a science club.

I shared my idea with my classmates. They, too, were bored stiff in the class but weren't in trouble academically as I was. They thought my idea superb. I suggested we begin a fund-raising project to acquire a telescope so we could observe the stars. Having convinced my classmates, I just had to convince Sister Marmion.

Sister was shocked at our interest, and she bought the

idea hook, line, and sinker. Given the green light, we organized a club, naming ourselves the name Moholettes, after
Mohorovicic discontinuity, the name for some god-forsaken
geological seismic wave related to the density of the mate-
rial in the earth's mantel that it moves through.

The boarders—students who lived on campus—bought
the bologna sandwiches we sold in our fund-raising efforts.
Selling anything we could get our hands on, we saved the
pennies, eventually getting enough money for the telescope.
What began as an attempt to save my grade, to deter Sister
from the boring subject she loved, and to convince her we
were brilliant, ended up, in the hands of Sister Marmion, as
a teachable moment.

She took the opportunity to teach us about seismic
waves in the earth and the science surrounding it. This was
just one example of how the nuns always seemed to find a
way to teach us, despite our best intentions to deflect the
lessons. And I must admit, we resisted their efforts almost
more than we gave in; the darker side of our nature surfaced
more times than I like to admit, causing more than one trip
to the confessional and the principal's office.

Most of our adolescent angst, though, was spent won-
dering what the sisters really looked like under their habits. Some had robust physiques. Others were extremely thin.
Our gossipy conversations yielded various descriptions, and
they always depended on the one doing the describing.

I found fascinating, intriguing, the life of the sisters—
cloistered, silent, prayerful, and trying to educate and train
over two hundred girls. Depending on the personality of
the student and the persona of the nun, most girls at Saint
Martin's had a favorite. My true favorite was Sister Maria
Goretti. First off, I liked her name, because I liked the saint

it referred too. Saint Maria Goretti, as a mere virginal child, stood against the sexual advances of her neighbor because of the love of her faith. She stood against the darkness of the human person. Maria was mortally wounded by the neighbor, Alessandro Serenelli, who attacked her with intent to sexually abuse her. He was twenty years old. Maria died the next day at the age of 11 years, 9 months, and 21 days, after forgiving Alessandro.

In those days after vows, nuns did not use their given names; instead, they would choose the name of a saint they wanted to emulate. After one of the many important searches we did as students, I found out that her given name was Eleanor. I preferred her chosen name. Maria Goretti had a livelier ring. She also had a brilliant mind and played the organ beautifully.

The real draw for me, though, was the way she carried herself: assured, strong, without apology or emotion. The first and only time we saw a hint of emotion was the day President Kennedy was murdered. We actually saw tears. We were shocked. Another plus was that she helped me get over some latent guilt I had when it came to saying the daily rosary; thanks to Mom and Father Peyton, I'd feel horrible guilt if I fell asleep before its completion. "Never worry," she said, "the angels finish it." Her kind response prompted me to thank God for her more than once; this woman saved my life.

The political bug found me at Saint Martin's. I ran for office twice, once for attorney general, once for sheriff. AMS (Annetta Marie Sanow) for SMA (Saint Martin's Academy). That was my campaign slogan. I won. Both times.

Saint Martin's dances, proms impacted the entire area. Saint Martin's girls invited young men from the local schools.

But our invitations often created problems. The boys loved it. Their hometown girlfriends did not.

I recall one particular dance. Well-lit hallways formed the stage as Sister David greeted our "dates" in the foyer. Sister sent one of the younger classmates to Sister Consuelo, who announced our names over the loudspeaker. Nervously, we made our way to Sister David. She greeted us in her gentle way and turned her "Saint Martin girl" over to the petrified boy.

We walked the well-lit hallway to the well-lit lunchroom, where the nuns surrounded the well-lit dance floor watching us "enjoy" our dances with our dates. There was no need to worry about moral lapses. We didn't stand a chance.

There were many memorable events—students from a North Dakota Catholic boys high school, on the road for a senior trip, were invited to spend an evening with us Saint Martin's girls. We were many. They were few. We wasted no time. We grabbed whomever we could, and quickly. Mine was from the Twin Cities. What a night. The evening came full circle many years later, when I bought a car from one of the twenty-five boys who visited that evening with over one hundred Saint Martin's girls.

I loved "Sister school." It fascinated me. I also felt accepted and safe with both the nuns and the girls—and with God as my guide. Scrupulosity, maybe even hyperscrupulosity, became a part of my life. I never passed a church without making a visit, for example. Churches were always open in those days, and I'd go in, bless myself, pray, and feel better.

Despite this kind of new habit, a smidge of defiance plagued me. The greatest defiance came when a group of girls began raiding the cafeteria. And one night, I was caught up in the plot. My early training for this night of plunder was my experience with Black Jack gum. Each thief had a responsibility. One person was on freezer duty, told to "Grab the fudgesicles." Another's goal was the refrigerator; she had been told, "Grab the fruit." The item of desire in the pantry was the cereal.

The nuns caught on. Sister Bernard was on patrol. No one messed with Sister Bernard. No one. All of us criminals had no idea who was waiting behind the metal table. Call it a miracle. Call it grace. Call it conscious. Or maybe it was fear. For some reason, I decided to remain in the dorm and be the "Watchwoman."

Three of the "saints" in our dorm had decided to go to the dark side. The term "saint" in our teenage vernacular meant a member of the National Honor Society, the Sodality. They were really good, intelligent girls. Straight-A students. Girls who never received a demerit, as I had. Some of them didn't even say bad words.

That night was their first attempt at crime. And everyone was busted by Sister Bernard. The wisdom, or maybe practicality, of the nuns played out when they sent saintly Sister David dorm room to dorm room to obtain confessions of the theft. "Girls, girls..." she began, in her sweet, melodious voice.

From our perspective, the number of criminals was so extensive that it seemed that the school would have to close. As a Sodality, class officer, and founder of the Moholettes, I had leadership skills, or so my dorm mates thought. They knew nothing of the incident with the Black Jack gum. I was the chosen one in our dorm to speak with Sister David. The first thing I did was apologize for our crimes, our sins. Secondly, I attempted to reason with Sister David, justifying our theft in the name of hunger. This was not totally true. It was just that many of the girls disliked the beef tongue and other such "delicacies," as the sisters called them, that we were served at meals.

Thirdly, I drew on the strong voice of Portia, whom I had portrayed in our school performance of Shakespeare's *Merchant of Venice*. "The quality of mercy is not strained. It droppeth as the gentle rain from heaven upon the place beneath." Sister David bought the three justifications, but not without punishment. We had to write out numerous times, "I will not steal."

Even in my apology and confession, Sister David knew I was full of it. She also knew that we were good kids with our mischievous sides. While meting out punishment, she maintained her gentle approach. And she stopped the crime spree. Of course, Sister Bernard's formidable presence had also placed the fear of God in us.

I wasn't quite Saint Jude, the patron saint of hopeless cases; the nuns taught me that reality. I knew that I wasn't perfect. But neither were they. They taught me many things: mercy; justice; a deep, rich faith; and a consciousness. This event returned me to the confessional.

At the time, I almost always carried a large prayer book packed with holy cards, and I prayed to them all. Saint Therese of the Little Flower and I were intimate friends, or so I thought. President Kennedy's soul flew to heaven over my daily praying to the memorial card handed out at Catholic Churches at the time of his death. May 29, his birthday, to this day is like a holy day.

"Tell Sister David the president's been shot," Father Joachim said to one of the sisters as my classmates and I passed him in the hallway on our way from Mass to lunch. There was with uncharacteristic emotion in the priest's voice.

The day he was murdered is etched in my mind. I could not eat. I rushed back to the dorm. As I opened the door, Walter Cronkite's voice came over the loud speaker: "President Kennedy has died at..." I fell to my knees, numb. The hallway filled with crying students and nuns. No one was exempt from the pain. I remember thinking, "Even Walter Cronkite's voice is different." From that moment forward, we lost our innocence.

I wrote a poem in which I attempted to capture my feelings for the man I followed since I was a fourth grader. I sent it to Jackie, Caroline, and John. It was contained in a book of poems I wrote for an assignment titled *Poems in Memory of JFK*. I received an A.

OUR LEADER
T'was the year 1917, on the 29th of May.
A hospital glowed on the bright spring day.
Joseph Kennedy was to become a father.
He knew one more would not be a bother.

The father wanted a daughter, the mother a son.
But they were both happy when it was all done.
The wee, little tot was named John.
Not Tom, Jim, Joe or Don.

John started to grow up fast.
Before he knew it, 1917 was in the past.
He was the skipper, on the PT 109,
A natural born leader, this was a sign.

Little did his mother know,
Her son would be president, this goes to show,

That when you are born, God has it planned,
To know just where and how you'll stand.

John Fitzgerald Kennedy was our man.
He was the leader of this land.
But in November of '63,
Someone shot him who could it be?

Some say Oswald, some don't know.
That only goes to show
The almighty God knows the one.
God also knows what he has done.
    —Annetta Sanow

"Do you want to help me serve the high school athletic association banquet at Saint Pat's?" Aunt Vi asked me when I was visiting her in Lead, South Dakota. It was one of my free weekends from Saint Martin's. I was a sophomore.

"Are you kidding?" I responded, nearly breathless. Visions of athletic jocks danced in my head. At the moment, I was an excellent example of how an all-girls school tends to bring out the animal in a female adolescent.

Even before we opened the door to the church basement, I could smell the cigarette smoke. It was the days when smoking was allowed just about everywhere. "Boy, those coaches sure do smoke," I said to my aunt. As I opened the door, the first thing I heard was laughter. The first thing I saw were pictures of Bill W. and Dr. Bob. At the time, I had no clue who the men in the pictures were. But my first thought upon hearing the laughter was, "I want what they have."

"I'm pregnant."

I snapped my head around. I had just arrived home from Saint Martin's for a holiday. The words had came from my mother's mouth.

"Mom!" I blurted out. The words she had spoken meant something terrible, terminal. We knew that, after Joey's birth, any subsequent pregnancy would be a terminal diagnosis.

She continued, "I am not afraid. If something happens—and I don't believe it will, but if it does..." She paused, her voice was calm. "If it does, you older girls can provide care for the baby and the two younger children."

The pregnancy took it's toll. Not on Mom, though. On Dad. He lived with the memories of Joey's birth and the fear of losing his first and only love. On April 23, 1964, Cecilia Ida Kittelson was born. It was Mom's easiest birth. She was forty-five years old. We called the baby Cece. If her siblings were ecstatic with the birth of Mary and Joey, they were beyond all life force about Cece's arrival. She was the perfect baby: beautiful, gentle, and loved by all.

In essence, she had four mothers, Mom, Karren, Vonnie, and me. Mary and Joe, young though they were, knew their lives would change and greeted it with joy. Cece became my little shadow. I kept her close every minute. Cece surfaced emotions in Vonnie I had never seen before. Vonnie worshipped her.

I looked up. I was home on vacation attending Mass. There he was. My heart stopped. Oh, my God. He was gorgeous. Tall and lean, wearing an athletic jacket with a big tiger, our school mascot, on the back. Patrick Joseph. The son of our superintendant. Eventually, my heart quieted, but not for long. He went to Communion, looked at me, and smiled.

I returned to Saint Martin's in love. That summer we dated. Abruptly, though, our dating stopped. He gave no explanation. I was devasted. We did not talk about it, although we travelled in the same group of friends, the nondrinkers and nonsmokers, throughout our senior year.

When we were dating, framed in our athletic numbers, we innocently had a number: his was fifty-two, mine, thirty-one. Our colors: his was blue, mine, green. Nicknames: his was PM, mine, AM. We received the class "outstanding senior boy and girl" awards. He played basketball and football. I, a cheerleader, cheered for him. All this, and yet I didn't know why we stopped dating. We did not discuss it for forty years.

Chapter 9

"Joey, what's wrong?" I asked. I found him crying in the corner.

He looked up, eyes brimming. "I am not in the wedding," he said.

The fall brought wedding planning. Our sister, Karren, was to become a bride. My little brother, Joey, at nine years old too big to be a ring bearer yet too small to be an altar boy, usher, or groomsman, felt left out of the planning for Karren and Dennis's big day.

I sat him on my lap and promised, "When I get married, Joey, you will be in my wedding. I promise." He was. In a red jacket, with a buzz haircut and big smile, and only eleven, he proudly walked guests to their pews. I was very protective of my little brother. I would have taken a bullet for him.

Years later, when it came to alcohol or being accepted because of his sexual orientation, though, I couldn't save him. As an adult, he came out to us girls. He felt safe. We loved him. We didn't flinch. The first one he told was my second daughter. The two were close. He felt safe coming out to Emy. Those who rejected, ridiculed him essentially destroyed him. He drank to numb the pain. Associated behavior and consequences followed.

⁓

None of us three sisters could—or would—ever forget.

Snuggled in a double bed, pillows propped up, blankets piled. Pepsi bottles sweating, three bottles waiting to be opened. Red licorice and sunflower seeds. (We called this menu "the usual.") Three blonde heads. Eyes smiling, never-ending giggles.

The only place, other than church, where I had ever felt safe after our first dad's death was between my two closest sisters. And it was about to end. It was our last night together. The next day, November 28, 1964, Karren would marry her high-school sweetheart, Dennis Lyle Fritz. She attempted to console us. It did not work. Vonnie, not prone to demonstrate emotions, became emotional. I wept openly. Others might have thought that her impending move with Dennis a few miles away didn't matter all that much. But for her two younger sisters, it was overwhelming.

⁓

Three sisters. We had shared a bed and bedrooms our entire lives. And we shared a promise, a childhood promise. Karren Elizabeth, big sister, tender advisor, nurturer, director, and younger sisters' cheerleader, revisited our childhood plan, the promise. She began, "With my wedding tomorrow, we will continue with our plan, our promise." It was the promise that we three sisters forged years before, sitting on the concrete wall in our backyard. Karren continued, "Tomorrow, Annetta, you are my maid of honor. Vonnie, the bridesmaid. At Annetta's wedding, Vonnie will be the maid of honor, I will be the bridesmaid." Her gentle voice went on, "At Vonnie's, I will be the maid of honor, Annetta, the bridesmaid. The two little girls will be flower girls, or junior bridesmaids." She was referring to our two youngest sisters, Mary and Cece. It was decided. Two years later, all plans were off.

~~~

In *Little Women*, Louisa May Alcott wrote of the death of Beth, one of the four sisters. As I read *Little Women*, my tears flowed without reserve, unaware of the reality soon to visit my sisters and me. First it would be Vonnie. Karren a year and half later. My beautiful sisters. Dead.

"Call Harry and LaVerna." It was a plea made often by the people of Corson County. This time, the plea was different. Their daughter lay on the street in front of the Legion Hall, so often the scene of community celebrations, dances, and Santa Claus Day. And this time, the plea was "Run and get Harry and LaVerna." Vonnie lay on the concrete only a block and half from home. She had been struck by a car driven by a popular high-school senior. We later were told that he had been drinking. At the time of the accident, no one checked. The sheriff and his deputy, the ministers with badges, her parents: tended to their injured daughter.

It was my junior year of high school. My best friend was dating the driver of the car that struck Vonnie. In fact, my friend was in the car. I was later told that the driver had been kicked out of practice because the director smelled alcohol on him. I don't know. I do know that my sister was hit two blocks from home. It altered our family. I was changed forever. He took away my maid of honor. My antagonist. My nemesis. My sister. My best friend. And my other best friend, the one who sat in the front seat that night, never again sat with me at Ma Schneider's and drank Pepsi, ate salted peanuts, or listened to "Bobbie's Girl" on the jukebox.

People said to me, "You should hate him." I never did. Forgiveness is not always easy, but it is always necessary.

~~~

The call had come the night after I returned to Saint Martin's from Easter vacation. The voice strident. It was my brother Wally's. "Annetta, Vonnie was hit by a car."

My response was quick. "No problem, Wally. Vonnie's tough." Thoughts raced through my mind.

"She will be fine." Wally continued, "We didn't want you hear it on the radio." Since Dad had a high-profile position in the state, Wally knew it could be reported without discretion. As if to convince himself, he continued, "You're right, she is going to be fine. We will keep you posted."

Twelve hours later, the next call came. This one was from Karren. I could barely make out her voice between the sobs. "Vonnie is gone. Annetta, Vonnie died." The phone booth closed in on me. My breath came in spurts. "No. No. No." I heard the words. They were coming from me.

Within seconds, I was surrounded by Saint Martin roommates. Sister Carol was there and uncharacteristically placed her arms around me.

"May her eternal soul rest in peace," she said. She was talking about my sister.

I gave her a pleading look. "Sister, please tell me it is not Vonnie. Please?" All she could do was hold me as all the girls surrounded the two of us, crying. Two of my best friends took me to Lead, where my aunt and uncle were waiting to take me home. Home without Vonnie.

As we drove to Lead, I looked down at my hand. The scar. It came from a fight Vonnie and I had over doing dishes. My mind raced. I could still feel the soft side of her butt cheek next to mine as we shared the toilet seat as little girls. Funny I thought of that.

My sister. My right arm. Dead. Two weeks before her sixteenth birthday. I had just seen her. Holy Thursday, Good Friday, Easter Sunday. Holy Week. Holy Time. The Last Time. We went to Shenandoah. Jimmy Steward, my favorite. The movie. Easter Sunday with Joe, her boyfriend, and Nick Nicksic, our childhood friend. No, she can't be.

"Vonnie, this can't be you." It was a voice crying in the desert. The words were mine as I saw her lying in the coffin. I tried to move her hair. Her beautiful blonde hair was always impeccable. Now it was lifeless. Overwhelming grief rushed through my body. Karren had Dennis. Wally, Barb. "And Vonnie, it was always you and me." I would never be the same.

The night she died, she wrote me a letter, sitting under the antique hair dryer from mother's long-closed beauty shop, drying her hair. She wrote, "Hi, Well guess I'll write a few lines mainly cause I have something to tell you. . . . I'm writing this letter mainly to thank you for everything you've done for Joe and me. If it weren't for you, he'd probably never looked my way again. No matter what happens, I have been happier than I have ever been."

Shirley had found the letter. The McIntosh ladies again showed up for us. Marge, Shirley . . . and the list went on. Shirley had found the letter when she was cleaning our bedroom.

The letter continued with various compliments, including a line stating she had always wanted to be like me. I was stunned. I thought, "I never knew she wanted to be like me. Vonnie, wanted to be like me?" If it were not in her own handwriting, I never would I have believed it.

The day she died, part of me died. Innocence died, and loneliness came to stay. Who would be there to share secrets? Whom would I make promises to? Who would fight for me? With me? Whom would I protect? Who would need my protection?

I don't remember her funeral. I was numb. I couldn't breathe. The day after the funeral, Mom said I had to return to Saint Martin's. Before I left I returned to the freshly mounded grave in Green Hill Cemetery. Vonnie was buried on the anniversary of Dad's death in Lemmon, in a plot by Grandma Bessie and Grandpa Ferd, Great-Grandma and Great-Grandpa Tracy, and Uncle Ferdie. Death, life, the importance of sisters, Catholic roots, and the terror of alcoholism; Vonnie's death taught me unknown life lessons at seventeen.

Our parish priest, Father John Birdsall, also the chaplain for the American Legion, wrote a column in their newsletter concerning Vonnie's death. Uncharacteristically angry, Father wrote about moral accountability and responsibility. He framed it in the context of Vonnie's death and what the community called an "accident." He wrote, "I believe that responsibility rests squarely on the shoulders and minds of every adult and teen-ager in this community. When, if ever will we begin to correct conditions that need correcting-never? If after an "accident" happens—and no accident ever just happens—it is caused by someone or something—then the ones involved have a grave duty, morally and civilly, to accept the responsibility involved."

The editor of the newsletter noted following Father's column; "For the benefit of any readers that may not understand what the above is all about. Just while we were having cake and coffee after the last meeting a car driven by a teenager hit a 15 year old girl on the street in front of the Legion Hall, she lived less than 10 hours after the 'accident.'"

———～———

Returning to Saint Martin's from the funeral, I was out of time. Father Lawrence, our high school chaplain and religion instructor, sat across the desk. Tall, partially bald, bespectacled, clad in his Benedictine robe, he welcomed me with a gentle voice. I had run out of time. I recited "The Hound of Heaven": the final test of a rocky semester with the gentle but firm priest. I could get through a few lines. But I only knew a few lines. Really, only the first three lines.

I began,

I fled Him, down the nights and down the days;
I fled Him, down the arches of the years;
I fled Him, down the Labyrinthine ways;

Fear gripped my already-exhausted body. Sweat seeped from my pores. I began to cry. Without skipping a beat, Father Lawrence gently began, "Annetta, you have been through so much. I plan to give you an A."

"What?!" My mind screamed. I was saved by my sister. Even in death, she protected me. It was a miracle. One of many. Then the storming question. "But in light of what happened, do I deserve it?"

"If one leaves, we *all* do," we told one another. "But we will make a promise. Every two years, we will have a reunion." I was leaving Saint Martin's, returning home to my grieving family a month after Vonnie's death. My grief expanded at the thought of leaving my Saint Martin's friends. I was leaving the friendships that for the past three years we had cemented by playing together, sharing our deepest dreams and secret crushes, and praying together. And now the seven of us were parting. But we made a promise. And we kept it.

For more than forty years, the girls whom the Benedictine nuns brought together remain friends, reuniting every two years. Catholicism teaches fidelity in many ways.

When I drove away for the last time from my beloved school, and my beloved friends, the cry of loss dug deep. Saying good-bye. It was torture.

My senior year, I returned to McIntosh and public school—without Vonnie.

Chapter 10

"If you will pardon a personal observation, I might add that I would be very pleased to have you enroll in our high school. I firmly believe that girls like you with high moral character and pleasant personalities add very much to the academic environment of the school." The letter closed with a "Sincerely," and was signed by our superintendent, my ex-boyfriend Patrick's father. The pleasant response followed a request for class requirements.

As my senior religion teacher, this same man talked about his story, including his faith and walk with sobriety. It was the first time I heard about how the disease of alcoholism had almost destroyed a life, had impacted a marriage and a family. I deeply respected him. And I felt the same about his wife.

The sudden change that had ended my romantic relationship with Patrick continued to hurt as I entered school that fall. We still travelled in the same group of friends without discussing the end of our romance.

Added to the return to public school was the fact that my grade-school classmates changed. So had I. I didn't fit. And for me, it was okay.

We exchanged a stolen look down the hallway of our high school. Our lockers were at opposite ends. I fell in love the first time I saw him. It was a certain something. And he wore wingtips. He liked spinach. Children followed him like the Pied Piper. Wing tips, spinach, and children: for me, all criteria for commitment. His name was Jack.

Smarting and confused from the sudden rejection of my summer love, Patrick Joseph, I was ripe for a new relationship. Jack's friend told me he liked me. I took the plunge. In a note, I wrote, "Will you go to the Sadie Hawkins dance with me?" Sadie Hawkins was the dance where the girls invited the boys. It was an invitation that changed my life.

The dance itself was indistinguishable from any other, really, except for the fact I was the only one who wore a dress (a vestige of the influence of the nuns). But that night began a relationship that lasted throughout my senior year. The rules that governed the behavior of athletes and cheerleaders in the school were strict. My parents' rules were stricter.

Not one to participate in extracurricular activities, Jack patiently waited for me after band concerts, choir and play practice, church services, home economics events, oratory contests, piano recitals, cheerleading, ball games, and a multitude of other activities, just to give me a ride the two blocks home. He'd lovingly kiss me, drive seventeen miles to his mother's farm, and do the same thing the next day.

Voted best driver in high school, Jack had driving skills that even my parents trusted. They allowed Jack to give my younger siblings a ride to school. In snowstorms, when the roads were blocked for days, his maroon Chevy, the lone vehicle coming down Main Street, meandered slowly through the snow banks, driving those seventeen miles to see me. Later, in our marriage, he never came home.

There was a first harbinger of trouble. Arriving at school one Monday morning, I ran into a friend who had been with Jack at a party the previous Saturday night. When I asked him about my friend's information—whether he had been at a party without me—he stated, "I wasn't there. They want to break us up." Unfortunately, the first part (that he hadn't been there) was a lie. The second statement (that people thought we should break up) was true. The locals knew Jack's patterns, I did not. I believed the lie, and there began a pattern: Jack's lying, my believing.

The symptoms of alcoholism include dishonesty, justification, and rationalization. If I had known the symptoms of addiction then as I do now, would I have heeded them? I don't know. I had never dated a boy who drank alcohol. Due to Dad's work, I valued staying away from alcohol. Yet, when it came to Jack, I did not heed the warnings. Consequences were coming.

"I crown you king of the dad's," I heard my home economics teacher say as she placed a crown on my father's head. My senior year of high school, I wrote an essay about how, although his blood did not run through my veins, this man was my dad, a giant of a man. He won. No one had to tell me he was a king. I knew he was. Some people called him my stepfather. No one said it to me the second time. He always referred to us as "his kids" or "our kids." To me, he was my dad.

I remained furiously loyal to both of my fathers, often telling people, "God gave me two dads: one in heaven and one here to take care of us." The only way that my parents treated Dad's chosen children differently than they did his biological children was that Dad gave my two younger sisters necklaces when they were married. On our wedding days, his two surviving older daughters never received a necklace.

The spring of my senior year of high school, I went college shopping. Dad took me to Mary College in Bismarck, North Dakota. It was Benedictine. And we also visited Presentation College in Aberdeen. I decided on Presentation. Several years later, I returned to graduate from and later teach at Mary College, now University of Mary.

"I want you to read this. Then we'll talk," Dad said, with an uncharacteristic pinched, concerned look on his face. It was the week following high school graduation. I was standing in the kitchen of our hotel on that warm summer day and had been preparing lunch for my younger siblings and the multiple men we boarded when he handed me a letter. The envelope and contents were addressed to my father, and the return address was that of Patrick Joseph's mother.

I looked at Dad quizzically. I knew the family was moving. It was a time of grief for me, since not only did I feel bad about the father of the family leaving our school system as superintendant, but I also loved their entire family, including the mother, the writer of the letter I was about to read. Why would their mother write my father a letter?

I removed the letter from the envelope and began to read. I saw these words: "She was the destroyer of our family."

She was apparently speaking about me, indicated that somehow their family was destroyed due to my relationship with her son and my being best friends with her daughter. The letter went on, with statements about my mother, my family, and me that struck me as obviously delusional. I was shocked. Stunned. It continued with cruel, savage defamation and desecration of my character.

Nausea hit, and my stomach churned with sadness. "I had no idea she felt this way," I stammered. Eyes brimming with tears, I looked up at my father.

He said, "She is sick, cruel, and does not know what she is saying." Dad said he had agonized about sharing the letter with me, feeling the same shock and surprise I had. However, he felt I had the right to read what she had written.

My father, as confused as I was but attempting to curb the pain, said, "Never write something you do not want someone else to read. This is an example of the pain it can cause." A creative side of me closed up that day. And my dad's advice began a conversation with what I later learned was my inner critic. I stopped writing. I had loved writing, penning pieces for my high school newspapers and yearbooks, writing poetry and prose. I squelched it all.

I gave that woman that kind of power over my life. I was devastated. "Is this why Pat stopped dating me?" I asked myself. Her letter silenced my pen until, while attending a writer's workshop in 1991 at Assumption Abbey in Richardton, North Dakota, taught by Kathleen Norris the granddaughter of Doc Totten, the doctor friend who tried to save Grandfather Ferd. Today she is a noted *New York Times* best-selling author, and she encouraged me to write, to tell my story. The inner critic began to rest. I picked up my pen. I began to write.

The letter from Patrick's mother was dated the day the family left our community. This stunning experience with Patrick and his family had repercussions throughout my life. The letter explained, at least in some indirect way, the reason her second son, after dating me, exchanging heart-throbbing love notes and gifts, and stirring the hope of both of us abruptly stopped. No explanation. Devastation. Common friends but no discussion. The rebound relationship was with Jack, that young man who became my husband and the father of my children.

~

The Presentation Sisters who had helped usher me into the world at McKennan Hospital now influenced my educational process. I entered my first year at Presentation College majoring in education. Arriving with Dad to the campus, I hadn't known that I was to be housed elsewhere, far from campus. Without a car, I also wasn't going to have access to public transportation or a shuttle van. There just wasn't any.

To compensate for the mix up and lack of communication, the school gave me the option of having a private room or a room with older, working students. I choose the private room. It became my refuge. The challenge of living in the college overflow several miles from the campus kept me from becoming well acquainted with college life. Daily, I walked the miles to the campus. The tree-lined streets with the manicured yards distinguished my college memories.

On the weekends, I went home, catching a ride back and forth on the mail truck whose driver smelled like Aqua Velvet aftershave and who had wandering hands. I knew that if I told my parents about this, my transportation would cease, keeping me in miserable isolation. I missed my younger siblings, home, and Jack.

"Will you marry me?" Jack asked as we drove down Main Street. No candles, romantic dinner, kneeling on bended knee. It was Thanksgiving weekend. He proposed in the maroon Chevy. I said yes. I knew a wedding was far in the future. But first I wanted to complete my degree. Fate had other ideas.

"Annetta, I am so proud of you," Karren had said the day I left for college. She always said words that made me feel whole. Karren Elizabeth Sanow Fritz, our Mother Theresa. We spent time together the weekends I returned home from college. She fed my spirit. She fed everyone's spirit.

The week prior to first-semester exams, Karren and Dennis were expecting their third child, and Karren was not feeling well. Mom asked if I would come home to help with the little ones: Karmon was two, and Jimmy, ten months. Without hesitation, I jumped on the mail truck, returning home to a sister under required bed rest.

It was a sacred time. Karren, as always, had a heart of purity. She always showed constant consideration of others, even at great expense to her own health. As I was cleaning, attending to her every need, she asked me to sit.

"Will you wear my wedding dress?" she asked.

I was stunned. Always pragmatic, she continued, "Three reasons: it will save money, we are the same size, and..." In a voice filled with emotion, she concluded, "And, I would be honored to have my little sister wear my dress." She designed her own wedding dress. It was made lovingly by Marge Katus. In its total simplicity, it was beautiful.

Sitting on the side of the bed, tears streaming down my cheeks as I looked in the eyes of my generous maid of honor, I said, "I am privileged you offered."

We had never talked about Vonnie's death. It was too painful. This gesture helped both of us remaining sisters.

Sunday night, saying good-bye to my sister, I had an overwhelming emotional breakdown. Karren usually understood my heart. However, this time, thinking it was my sadness about leaving Jack and returning to school, she guessed wrong. I was unable to tell her of my sadness about leaving her. I had some sense that if I were to stay and take care of her, she would be fine. Later that night, she was taken to the hospital.

She was then transferred to a larger hospital where, after three days, she was diagnosed with a ruptured appendix. Multiple doctors had diagnosed her with false labor. They had been wrong. First, the baby she was carrying, only four months into gestation, died. Then peritonitis set in. Karren fought to live, hanging on to the thread of life. Dennis and Mom kept vigil. Dad drove the one hundred eighty miles between Saint Alexis Hospital in Bismarck and home, trying to tend to his family and the people of his county. I, too, took care of things at home, including Karren's little ones and my younger siblings. Two days later, my sister died.

The infection killed her. Her husband, her family, and the entire community were crippled with grief.

A little over a year after Vonnie's death, Karren Elizabeth Sanow Fritz was gone. The loss of one so good left a two-year-old, a ten-month-old, and the love of her life without a mother and a wife. The rest of us were left without the heart of our family. At her funeral, Father John Birdsall expressed what we all felt when he read from the Book of Wisdom 3:1–7.

"I am sure," he began, "that this reading reflects the sentiments of the family and relatives of Karren, and of the community, as it does so well my own, concerning her life, her suffering, and her death. The personal example of encouragement that we have had the privilege of having in our midst in the life and death of Karren Fritz has been a gift. She has shown in her generosity a union with Christ through the example of Christian witness. Devoted to her family, loving wife to her husband, and generous mother to her children, she was a willing witness to Christ in her work among the little children of our parish. She was truly the valiant woman of which the Book of Proverbs speaks: 'A perfect wife, who can find her? She is far beyond the price of pearls. Her husband's heart has confidence in her. From her he will derive no little power.'"

Father's homily captured the essence of this remarkable woman. Karren was without guile. She was tender and loving without reserve. She loved us. She loved her children. She adored Dennis. Karren was twenty-one years old.

Concluding Karren's funeral homily, Father stated, "If I may be permitted one more thought? May we all take notice of the courage and faith of the family—and of Karren's husband, Dennis, in the face of this tragedy, which is certainly no stranger to any one of them personally or professionally. May I offer sympathy and condolences, as well as gratitude, personally and on behalf of the congregation and the community. I know that their example on this occasion will be a source of strength and courage to us all."

We had strength and courage. However, this time it was at great cost. After the deaths of the Vonnie and Karren, Mom changed. We all did. Our oldest brother began to drink. Added to the reality of the situation was the fact that the one daughter from Mom's first marriage, the daughter with whom she struggled, was still alive.

As I had decided to leave Saint Martin's after Vonnie's death, I decided to leave Presentation College after Karren's. Mom, Dad, and Dennis needed help with the babies.

I found my boyfriend, Jack, supportive of me through this tragedy, although a few weeks after Karren's death he was charged with providing alcohol to a minor. While that was a common occurrence in my hometown, nevertheless I heard about it from other people and had a difficult time ascertaining what really happened.

Several versions of the story surfaced. The incident with the minor had apparently occurred prior to Karren's death, while she was in the hospital dying. Charges were filed later. Dad and I were called to testify. At the time, of course, our family was in a fog, trying to pull together some order, some normalcy. I was numb. During this period, I made critical decisions that would affect me for all the days to come. I offer no excuses and take full responsibility for my own decisions, but I know that grief played a significant role in the decision I was about to make.

Chapter 11

The following June, I went ahead and married Jack. Due to the alcohol charge against him and her grief, my mother no longer supported my plans to marry Jack. It was the perfect storm. Mom's and my relationship did not emerge whole. Rather, the events submerged it. It was a formidable moment that further fueled her dislike of me. Monsignor Leahy stepped in to give pastoral care to Mom and me. Dad reached out to me with his characteristic understanding. Jack remained neutral. He did not want my parents to dislike him, especially Dad.

At nineteen years old, I was confused and afraid, both of going through with the marriage and of what would happen if I didn't. Instead of a time of joy and anticipation, my wedding preparations were scarred by the losses of my two beloved sisters, as well as tension. Death had negated our childhood plan. My maid of honor and bridesmaid were gone. Lovingly, Dennis encouraged me to honor Karren's wish to wear her dress.

On June 1, among family and friends, Jack and I were married at Saint Bonaventure, the place of many sacramental celebrations. I stood in the same place where, only months before, my sisters' coffins had sat. And in truth, my wedding was more like a funeral. In Karren's dress, I walked down the aisle on the arm of the man who raised me. He, too, was crying.

As I prepared to leave on my honeymoon, Karmon, my two-year-old niece, held on to me. I was yet another person leaving her little world. It rent my heart. The memory of it still does.

The day was bittersweet. Our honeymooning began in Lemmon forty miles from home, where our motel reservations were waiting. Dairy Queen the only available alcohol-free eating establishment open to underage newly weds, so we began our married life with hot dogs and french fries. It matched the romantic proposal. My wedding gift from my husband was a Chihuahau. He liked dogs.

Traveling to the stunning Black Hills of South Dakota, we spent time exploring, enjoying our new life. We visited friends, as well as Aunt Vi, Uncle Jim, and my cousins, who were always balm for my soul. Two days before we were to return home, news flashed on television screens across the nation: Robert Kennedy had been shot. I wanted to go home.

Jack did not understand. The Kennedys for me were like family. Bobby Kennedy, like Jack, had shaped my life when I was a young child. I began following John when he ran for Senate. President Kennedy's assassination impacted everyone. For me, it was intense. Now Bobby. I prayed that God would keep him alive. We returned home to the news of his death. Jack didn't care. He was not happy about coming home a day early.

I decorated and organized our home. I loved every minute of making what I felt was a little nest for my husband. The house was transformed to a dollhouse. The aroma of freshly baked caramel rolls, bread, and a multitude of foods made with deep love was a daily fare. After two weeks of marital bliss, I saw Jack less and less. Beautifully prepared meals became cold as I waited for him to come home. At this time, he wasn't drinking, but he returned to our home at varied times, always without explanation.

Suddenly, nothing felt certain. Confused by the abrupt change in our relationship and extremely naïve, I felt it must be something I was doing wrong. I baked more, cooked different recipes, and kept an even more spotless house.

"You are the brunt of jokes. They talk about you and make fun of you and your church," Jack's niece told me after Jack and I had been married a few of months. She wanted to protect me and so told me what was occurring in Jack's family. I didn't realize it, but she now was my only ally. Prior to this moment, I knew in the midst of Jack's family, a saint resided. She was Susie Henderson Hendrickson, his grandmother. Truly a saint. I knew she loved me. I adored her. Her apron was a big as her heart. She died shortly after we were married.

"You are the topic of ridicule, jokes, and cruel remarks. They make fun of your spotless house. They laugh about bringing their kids over to mess it up and think it's funny. They laugh about your cooking and baking," she said. But most of the ridicule, she reported, involved my religion and belief system. Every Catholic knows some people who are anti-Catholic. We are raised with it. Certainly I had been exposed to it before. But this was different.

Something happened to me at that moment. Naiveté does not capture the reality. I simply could not understand their feelings. They saw my generosity of hearth, home, and heart as a character defect. I was stunned people could be so cruel. I loved Jack's family. To know they felt very differently about me crushed me.

I held the pain close to my heart. I felt alone. How could I be so stupid? Had Mom been right to object to my marrying Jack? Was Jack taking part in the ridicule? Did his need for acceptance from his family motivate him to turn against me? I did not know. He did not tell me. I felt alone, unable to share my feelings with anyone. A keen observer, Rachael, my older and wiser neighbor, knew Jack's family and saw what was happening. She attempted to help by talking to Jack.

Now the only place I felt safe, accepted, and normal was at church. It was my lifeline. This reality never changed during the ten years of our marriage.

"Yes," Doctor Lorenzen said. "You are pregnant."

"Pregnant?" I thought. "I am pregnant?" I don't know why it never occurred to me that I could become pregnant just a few months into marriage, but it didn't. I guess it was due to the fact that I had been brought up with Sister Marsha and Father Falkin's sex education class. As I look back, I realize that, at the time, I was truly clueless—"stupid" is probably a better word—about all things sexual. No one had talked to me about it, including Mom and Karren.

Jack was excited and happy about the news. But he told me we should keep it to ourselves, because his family would not understand. I knew he was right. It would only give them more fodder for more ridicule. But I told the world anyway. I was ecstatic.

Soon after, Jack told his brother that he and I needed to move or his mother and sister were going to destroy me. He was right. Rachael's talk had worked. I was hopeful and thought that perhaps the joy of a child would change what was happening.

We moved to a ranch. There, our marriage thrived as we anticipated the birth of our first child. We lived and worked on the same ranch as did Jack's brother Jim and Jim's family. I loved our nephew and nieces. Weekly, I travelled the seventy miles to McIntosh to continue giving piano lessons to the students I had begun teaching prior to our move. It also was a wonderful excuse to see my family. I missed Mom, Dad, and my siblings.

Jack and I worked well together. Like Grandma Bessie, I started to can vegetables, meats, and fruits. Homemade bread became my specialty. I loved ranch living, especially during the spring. It was calving time, the opportunity to experience new life.

If a heifer died during birthing or did not nurse the calf, we fed it. More than once, we brought a calf to the house, warming it in the bathtub. I related to all of the soon-to-be mother cows. We all were preparing to calf. I found, as many did before me and many will after, that ranch and farm life brings you close to all that is life giving.

Life was good.

"It's a girl," the doctor announced.

It was a miracle. The birth of our first daughter, Amy Marie, named for Dad's sister Amelia. It was my first true experience of the Divine. I felt as though my heart would burst. My sweet baby's father, with tears of flowing down his cheeks, held her tiny body, just over five pounds of sheer joy.

That moment began a special relationship between father and daughter. I knew from the moment of her birth that theirs would be a special relationship. I smiled, watching them. We were now a family.

"We have too much love for one child," Jack said as we hovered over our little one. He was correct. Our love was immense and deserved to be shared with more.

"Chocolate. Please?" I responded when Jack asked me if I need anything from town. Six weeks after Amy's birth, my craving for chocolate had not subsided. Jack had offered to drive the five miles to town to get me a treat. But he did not return when he should have. The clock ticked away: two hours, three, four. . . .

My first fear was a car accident. We had one vehicle. His brother and family were gone. I worried. I prayed. I cried. I saw lights coming down the road. Finally, it was our canary yellow Ford. It was one thirty in the morning. I was so relieved.

He came into the house drunk. He tried to get to the bedroom. He fell. I tried to help him. At over six feet tall, he was too much for me. I struggled. Finally, I was able to help him to the bottom end of the bed. Shortly after, he began to throw up. I turned him on his side to keep him from aspirating. The vomit was lime green. He told me later he had been drinking lime vodka. He explained, "I began visiting with an older man at the bar who kept buying me drinks."

I excused the event as a hard-working, young, new father needing a few moments to himself. A knot began to form in my stomach. Alcoholism began its ugly cruel ascent in our home. That night began a pattern of alcohol use, abuse, and horror. He forgot the chocolate. Never again did my husband bring me chocolate.

"We're moving," Jack announced. We did. Then he made the same announcement again.

The geographical change continued. After a couple of more moves and four different jobs, Jack wanted to leave the area and start a new life. He wanted to fulfill his desire to become a law enforcement officer like his idol, my father. Our move to the eastern part of the state helped him achieve it; first, he became a city police officer. By the time he was twenty-five years old, Jack had been promoted to chief of police.

He was responsible for the entire city. Then he began to experience chest pains. One time as we rushed him to the hospital, fear lodged in my throat. A heart attack. I flashed back to my father. I was terrified.

After examining Jack, the doctor provided him with a cure. "Jack," he said, "take a drink after work; it will relieve the pain and relax you." The doctor explained to us that stress was causing the muscles around Jack's heart to constrict. I was stunned. In my eyes, the doctor had just given him permission to kill himself.

And so after his shift, Jack drank. When I made any attempt to discuss what was happening, Jack referred me back to the words of the doctor.

We continued to move. During the ten years of our married life and the growth of our family, we moved eleven times. Between pregnancies and packing, my life was filled with loving the children, cooking, cleaning, and hugging, and it was all wrapped in prayer and church.

In the earlier years of our marriage, Jack was willing to

spend money on alcohol before spending it on necessities for Amy, at the time our only child, and household expenses. Money became an issue. To help with finances, I started a day-care center in our home. I loved it. Amy was one year old. Loneliness in our marriage was becoming constant. In fact, the loneliness and isolation were repressive.

Our parish priest came to visit, and he tried to help me. He encouraged me to begin a youth program in the parish. I did. And I played organ for Sunday Mass. To a large extent, motherhood kept joy in my life. As did church. So I played the organ with Amy by my side and spent time developing the youth program, again with Amy by my side.

The good moments with Jack, although few and far between, were wonderful. On Jack's days off, we went fishing. Amy loved it. She sat right beside her father as they wormed the hook and threw it in. I loved watching the two of them. At that time, Jack only drank after his shift was over. He was not a bar drinker.

Then, I discovered I was pregnant.

Emy Patrice joined her sister, Amy, on May 15. We named her after Grandma Emelia Schultz Sanow who, like my father, I never really knew. I wanted the connection. I wanted our daughter to feel it, too.

She was a beautiful child, with large, lovely eyes. She and her sister became inseparable. They reminded me daily of Vonnie and me. Emy became her father's shadow. She loved being with her dad. I recall one really poignant moment watching Emy run to find her father.

"Dad? Dad!" Emy would call out. He'd turn and take her with him.

At first I marveled at how she knew the precise moment

when he left the house. Then Jack and I figured it out. Jack's habit when returning home from work was to place his cap on the top of the refrigerator. "Watch," Jack said to me one day, as he placed his baseball hat in his usual spot on the refrigerator. He stood around the corner and with his mischievous smile, reached around and took down the hat. Emy came racing through and ran to the door to find her dad. He caught her in his arms, and the two began to laugh. The laughter filled the house. She was safe in her father's arms.

The man I fell in love with was changing. So was I. After the birth of our second daughter, things began to drift to a place of darkness. My lifelong dream had been to have a house filled with children born from a man I love and who loved me, providing a home filled with gentleness and security. This dream was quickly slipping away.

A cycle of physical abuse began. The violence always began when Jack was drinking. First, it was a push.

"I want that money," Jack yelled.

"Jack, it is for the rent," I responded. But it didn't matter that the rent was due. He took it anyway. And he took my well-being with every shove.

Tension built. He tried to fix what he had done. Reconciliation followed the violence. Then we'd moved back to the place of tension. It became a cycle, most of the time ending and beginning without any remorse on Jack's part.

Fighting and nagging were not in my temperament. I cried. Later, I'd discover that he did not know or remember what he had done or said. Often he was essentially anesthetized. In a blackout. I'd remember the vile words coming from the mouth of the man I loved. I'd remember the pushes. Most of the time he didn't.

I spent significant time attempting to hide what was occurring in our home. I was terrified. The first crack in my isolation occurred when I shared the situation with our parish priest. He listened. He encouraged me to take some action. I was scared.

But soon after, I could not take it anymore. The two little girls and I moved back to my parents' house. It was during this time of separation that my father did an intervention on Jack. He took him to the state hospital in Yankton. It was the first of many treatment processes.

This first time, he returned clean and sober. We reconciled. For a month and a half, we had our life was back. It was like a second honeymoon. And then he did not come home from work one night. I panicked and called his counselor at the state hospital. He asked me, "Do you watch for the headlights to come home? Is it difficult to swallow food? Is your pillow wet from crying?"

I thought, "My God, this man is living with me."

"Yes to all of those things," I responded.

Then he said, "Whether you realize it or not, Annetta, you are as sick as Jack."

"I don't even drink," was my rapid response.

"That is part of the problem; you have nothing to numb your feelings. Jack does. He is numb all the time," he explained. For the first time I heard the words that later changed my life: "Go to Al-Anon."

I didn't listen. Jack stayed in the relapse. And I became pregnant.

~~~~

Her name was Ruth. Ruth K. We were sitting in her beautiful, spotless, well-organized kitchen, stuffing envelopes. The usually reserved woman I looked upon as a role model for women asked, "Can I ask you a personal question?"

Eager to respond, I quickly said, "Ask me anything."

She continued, "Are you concerned about Jack's drinking?" She held up her hand, as if to stop a response. "You don't have to answer. I want you to knows something: you remind me of me." Stunned, I listened as she told me her story.

"Al-Anon," Ruth said, "saved my life." This was the second time within weeks I had heard of Al-Anon. She continued, "I cannot tell you what to do. I can tell you what Al-Anon had done for me."

That day, I heard Ruth's words. But time lapsed before I heeded her suggestion. Not until June 10, 1975, did the suggestion ripen.

~~~~

On January 30, 1974, Jenny Jo—our little princess, as we called her—was born to us delighted parents and her two loving sisters. With her big sisters, she completed the trinity. Amy, Emy, Jenny. Karren, Annetta, Vonnie. Again, Jack's tears streamed down his cheeks as he looked at the little beauty.

A day after her birth, doctors discovered a heart defect. "I am referring her to Minneapolis. They are equipped to do the necessary tests," the gentle doctor said. I felt as if a vice grip was choking me. I called Jack. He returned to the hospital immediately. I asked for a priest. Father Eugene Frank was visiting a patient in the hospital. We baptized her.

Prior to her birth, I had asked our long-time family friend Leona Senftner to be the new baby's godmother. She came to the hospital.

"I want you to have this," she said as she handed me an envelope before we left for Minneapolis. She understood much about my life, having firsthand knowledge of living with the disease of alcoholism. I began to sob. We had no money for the trip. I had told no one. And now the woman from whom I had stolen a pack of Black Jack gum as a child was providing the funds.

I was unable to concentrate with the thought of our baby having tests, perhaps heart surgery. I was unable to sleep. I prayed. Jack got drunk. The doctor reported that it was a hole in her heart. Infancy, at that time, prohibited surgery. "It will take time," he said. "We will continue to observe. Watch her fingernails. If they turn blue, take her to the hospital immediately."

The hospital was seventy miles from our home. And her father was an alcoholic.

"Hail Mary, full of grace. . . ." Each night I blessed my baby with holy water as I held her tight and prayed that the hole in her heart would close. Her two sisters lay nearby, unaware of the seriousness of their sister's condition.

Another reality was beginning to take shape.

My mother had always been a teetotaler. I had never seen this woman take a drink. Never. Quiet the opposite. She had stood against the onslaught of alcohol and supported anyone who tried to address it, a stance that was rare in those days.

Mom and Dad had a unique vantage point, due to their positions in law enforcement. They had pulled bodies from

August & Emelie Shultz Sanow.

Ferdinand "Ferd" & Elizabeth "Bessie" Tracy Braun.

Sanow Family Farm.

Braun Family Farm.

The fire in Lemmon, South Dakota Ferd Braun & Bill Stoick moments before the train hit Ferd.

LaVerna Braun Sanow Kittelson.

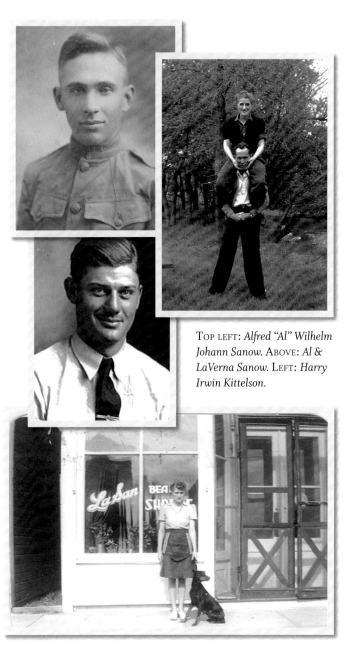

TOP LEFT: *Alfred "Al" Wilhelm Johann Sanow.* ABOVE: *Al & LaVerna Sanow.* LEFT: *Harry Irwin Kittelson.*

La San, Mom's first salon.

LEFT: *Sanow children prior to their father's death.*
BELOW: *Year after Dad's death.*

Harry & LaVerna Kittelson.

LEFT: *Early McIntosh, South Dakota deemed 'Best Town in State.'* BELOW LEFT: *Our first family picture with 2nd Dad.* BELOW RIGHT: *Favorite picture of Wally, the protector.*

After Mary's birth, in the dreaded brown stockings & saddle shoes.

LEFT: *Father Szealy and me.*

MIDDLE AND BOTTOM: *Jimmy Erz and me always side by side.*

ABOVE: *Dakota Hotel with new remodel.* RIGHT: *Vonnie 'first female priest' in Father Szealy's collar.*

American Legion Hall, McIntosh—home of joy and sadness.

Sheriff Harry I. Kittelson.

1962 Spring Band Concert last time together.

Saint Martin's Academy.

CLOCKWISE FROM TOP: *Beloved sisters Karren Elizabeth Sanow Fritz; LaVone 'Vonnie' Patrice Sanow; Saintly Sister David.*

ABOVE: *Jack and Annetta and the wedding dress.*
RIGHT: *Karren and Dennis Fritz and the wedding dress.*

Our first family picture: Jack, Annetta, and our three daughters.

TOP: *Amy, Emy, Jenny, Chet, and Bret.* ABOVE: *Chet Patrick 3lbs 15½ oz.* LEFT: *Our first official family picture.*

Top: *The last family photo shortly before Dad's death.*
Middle: *Siblings Wally, Joe, Mary, Annetta, and Cece.*
Bottom: *The grandchildren carrying Grandpa Harry.*

Saint Irene Erz, Jimmy's mom visiting with me at Dad's funeral.

ABOVE: *Wally and me on our last trip together.* RIGHT: *The picture of me that Mom had left on the buffet the last day of her life.*

RIGH: *The night of the alumni award at U of M.* BELOW: *My family prior to all leaving home.*

LEFT: *Emerson Joseph and me at Mother Teresa's children home-Haiti.* BELOW: *Turning rape to legislation.*

TOP: *Sanow family reunion on the Sanow farm Cherokee Co. Iowa;*
BELOW: *Saint Martin's friends reuniting;*

TOP TO BOTTOM: *My beautiful family; Grandma's joy; My children Amy, Emy, Jenny, Bret (missing: Chet Patrick).*

the carnage, identified bodies maimed and mutilated, notified families of tragedy, and counseled countless people on
what drinking was doing to them and their families.

Often, they protected and provided necessities to the
children who had been abused, neglected, or abandoned
by drinking parents. Yet neither she nor Dad ever came to
understand alcoholism as a disease. Their patience in these
circumstances was extraordinary—up to a point. And when
that point was reached, it came with a price. Anger. Mom's
anger. She'd be swept along by an overwhelming anger
about those neglected, abused, abandoned children, no matter what the cause. Dad was more passive.

"Drink this; it may help," urged a family friend after the
death of one of my sisters. Mom took the drink. Immediately
it became a problem, albeit one unnoticed and denied by
most in our family until she experienced a major blackout.
Then my mother stopped as she started: cold turkey.

By this time, I was already living with Jack's active alcoholism. Watching Mom and experiencing what was occurring
in my own little family, I became keenly aware of how the disease of addiction can happen at any time in life, due to complicated realities, genetic predisposition, and the pain of loss.
I also began to witness what I later learned is the difference
between sobriety and recovery: you can be sober and miserable or in recovery, working a spiritual program of recovery,
serene and happy. Mom and Jack were doing neither.

While Mom and Jack never drank together, he was asked
more than once to buy alcohol for her. Mom's drinking took
her to another level of protracted disgust toward me. The
things that were said and done during those years are too
painful to recount. Two of the most important people in my
life were drinking. I was breathing, but not living. "*Io non*

more, e non rimasi vivo," (I did not die, yet nothing of life remained) said Dante in the *Inferno*. An inferno was suffocating me. I needed help.

Maybe Ruth and Jack's counselor from the state hospital had been right. I called a number for information about Al-Anon. A nice voice said, "Yes, we have a meeting at eight o'clock at Saint Mary's Catholic Church, in Lemmon, South Dakota. It's held in the basement. Just go to the door and someone will help you."

Chapter 12

The copper handle was weathered from years of hands reaching for it. The hinges bent to the door's weight as I opened it. My stomach churned. Saint Mary's Church. Lemmon, South Dakota. The same church. Mother's baptism, First Communion, and confirmation, and the funerals of her beloved parents, as well as those of two of the five brothers. It was where she and her brothers had received their early education. It was in this sacred place and the convent across the street that the nuns gave piano lessons to Mom's children. To me.

The door opened. I heard voices. Laughter. Softened, compassionate responses. I began to turn away. "No," I said to myself, as if I needed convincing. "I am doing this."

I walked down the steps, toward the voices. I turned and walked back up. I walked back down. For some reason I couldn't move forward. Was it fear? I counted the steps. Twelve. I went back up. Back down. Still twelve. Finally, after a journey of a thousand miles and counting the twelve same steps I don't know how many times, I opened the door. The room was full of women.

The first one next to the door reached her hand out with a gentle smile. "Hi, my name is Mildred. Welcome to Al-Anon." My legs were shaking, my heart, pumping. I sat down.

The woman I sat next to squeezed my hand and said the same wonderful word. "Welcome." The tears welled in my eye. Another woman began to read, "Welcome..." Although the words that followed seemed to be in a foreign language, I found them soothing, a balm for my wounded spirit.

She asked if there were any newcomers. I cautiously raised my hand. Another gentle welcome. It was too much. I began to weep uncontrollably. They just said the soon-to-be-familiar words, "We're glad you're here." Love was offered, not imposed.

I was home. My life forever changed that June 10, 1975. June 10, my biological father's birthday. A picture sitting on the literature table that first night grabbed my eye. It was the same pictures that watched over the AA conference all those years ago at Saint Patrick's Church. They were of Bill W. and Dr. Bob.

The night began a lifelong connection to Bill W. Those two men and their wives, Lois and Anne, were about to transform my life. Later I learned another significant event occurred on June 10. It was Dr. Bob's sobriety date. Dr. Bob: the cofounder of AA. My arrival that day was fitting. For me, the coincidence of dates was a spiritual sign.

I was handed two books. One said *Alcoholics Anonymous*. The other, *One Day at a Time in Al-Anon*. I devoured—no, inhaled—the books. First the Al-Anon book. Then *Alcoholics Anonymous: The Big Book*. They were filled with the language of the heart.

We had alcoholism in our home. I learned it was a brain disease, not a moral failing. A progressive disease. We had been ignorant of what was happening. Breath returned to my body. Feeling like a ship wrecked, I was offered a life raft. Stunned, I realized, "We are good people, Jack and I, with a disease, a bad disease permeating our home. And we can get well." I found later that this statement wasn't quite true. I could get well. I could not make another well.

When I was handed *Alcoholics Anonymous: The Big Book*, it was like rain to parched earth. I no longer feared the disease. I embraced it. I could get well. I knew the problem. Now I had a solution. Jack did, too, if he were willing.

I had known religion, understood the gift of faith. With recovery, I experienced spirituality. I finally and truly understood the difference between religion and spirituality. For me, the two, although different, are interconnected. The ultimate act of faith is to believe in the light, even in the darkness. With the glimmer of this realization, I began embracing the twelve-step way of life.

The American Medical Association in 1956 proclaimed alcoholism an illness. In 1966, alcoholism was identified as a disease. Ultimately, science has shown that addiction is a physical disease of the brain caused by exposure to drugs. Still, to this day, the issue is debated. However, no one debates the impact of addiction on the spirits of the drinkers and their family members.

The history of AA became a fascination, a passion, for me. I read everything written: how, where, when. I learned of the early Catholic influence in Bill Wilson's life. In his childhood, he had been surrounded by churches. His family church, a congregational church, was an arms length from the Wilson home, a Catholic church, with a row of trees separating them, not far behind.

I love the stories of the two pivotal Catholics who walked

with Bill W. and Dr. Bob in their quiet pastoral ways. The Catholic influence in AA, like much in the mystery of recovery, came off the streets of New York City. Bill W., in one of his dark nights of the soul, full of exhaustion, lingering depression, and the desire to bring the program of recovery to an unwanting world, heard one more knock on the door. It was old Tom, the maintenance man. Bill learned that "some bum from Saint Louis" was there to see him.

In his exhaustion, Bill muttered, "Not another one." He laid aside the thought. "Send him up," he told Tom. Assuming by the sound of uneven steps that the visitor was intoxicated, Bill steeled himself for the talk. Opening the door, he realized the man suffered from a physical challenge. He later found out that it was crippling arthritis. The two men presented their right hands to one another.

When the man removed his raincoat, Bill recognized the collar of a Roman Catholic priest. "I am fascinated by the article Jack Alexander printed in the *Life* magazine about these twelve steps, Bill," the man said. He continued, "I am a Jesuit. The Jesuits live their lives based on the exercises of Saint Ignatius."

Bill was unaware of anything Jesuit.

"The twelve steps are similar to the exercises," the priest explained.

Talking over the next few hours forged a friendship between these two men that lasted the rest of their lives. Bill W. met what Catholic's call grace in the person of the Father Ed Dowling. Bill W. called Ed Dowling the spiritual director of AA. He became one of the only nonalcoholic members of the first board of directors. Considered a fringe person in his religious order by his confreres, Father Ed understood the loneliness of the dispossessed alcoholic.

The similarities between the twelve steps and Ignatian spiritual exercises are startling: decision, daily examination, contemplation, examining sin (the separation of a person in his or her relationship with God, self, and others), taking responsibility, making amends, prayer and meditation, humility. The steps, as do the exercises, help us embrace the gift of creation within the human person; they help us fill the spiritual hole.

The second critical Catholic in AA's early history was Sister Ignatia. Dr. Bob worked with Sister Ignatia, a frail, Irish American, no-nonsense nun and admission director of Saint Thomas Hospital in Akron, Ohio, who shaped the hospital concept of treating alcoholism as a medical issue. She began by first secretly detoxing alcoholics in the hospital's garden room. She was "forced" to do this—she had little choice—because alcoholism wasn't accepted as a disease and people had little compassion for alcoholics.

Today, because of this little nun and other brave, compassionate, strong pioneers, alcoholics are brought through the front doors of hospitals and treatment centers with the dignity of any human suffering from a chronic disease. Due to Sister Mary Ignatia Gavin not backing down, alcoholics are treated like anyone suffering from a chronic, progressive disease.

Sister Ignatias gave her newly five-day detoxed alcoholics Sacred Heart medals, charging them with the responsibility of returning it if they were going to drink. Thus began the tradition of giving and receiving medallions to celebrate the milestone of an AA member's sobriety and the length of sobriety.

Bill had Father Ed. Bob had Sister Ignatia. AA needed these Catholics. Catholics need AA. Much later, another priest, Father Joseph M., the beloved recovery priest, also was a recovery trailblazer, with his groundbreaking film "Chalk Talk on Alcohol." He was a giant in the field of chemical addiction and recovery. He too, impacted millions. It was through his suffering from the disease of alcoholism and his subsequent recovery that he was able to love. Many Catholic alcoholics often quote him: "Where two or three Catholics are gathered there also is a fifth." Through his words, Father Joseph M. continues to speaks to the reality of how much Catholics need AA.

Another example of Catholic influence included in the history of AA is Bill W.'s favorite prayer, the prayer of Saint Francis of Assisi, who, too, knew rejection, ridicule, and isolation and turned it to grace by loving others, both people and animals. It is reprinted in AA's *Twelve Steps and Twelve Traditions*, written after *Alcoholics Anonymous: The Big Book*.

PRAYER OF SAINT FRANCIS OF ASSISI
Lord, make me an instrument of your peace.
Where there is hatred, let me sow love;
Where there is injury, pardon;
Where there is doubt, faith;
Where there is despair, hope;
Where there is darkness, light;
And where there is sadness, joy.

O, Divine Master, grant that I may not so much seek
To be consoled as to console;
To be understood as to understand;
To be loved as to love.
For it is in giving that we receive;

It is in pardoning that we are pardoned;
and it is in dying that we are born to eternal life. Amen.

Why this connection between Catholicism and AA?

Catholics are no better and no worse than others. However, our foundation and traditions speak of the spiritual journey to God. In the steps of AA that understanding is expanded for the recovering person to find a power greater than themselves. For many people that source is God. For others it is the Great Spirit, Allah, nature or the group of recovering people.

~

I found out at the first meeting the only requirement for membership in AA is a desire to stop drinking. For Al-Anon membership, the only requirement is to have a family or friend impacted by alcoholism. Twelve-step programs thrive on anonymity. Why? Because your presence is protected. Only first names are used with none of the titles. No matter who, what, or how you came through the door of AA or Al-Anon your anonymity is protected. If you choose to share it outside the meeting, that is up to you. Anonymity is one of the traditions. Everyone is the same: no more, no less. I found the program of AA so simple that it seemed to defy logic. Today, it is often dismissed because of the simplicity. In recovery, I found that I became stronger and found my voice. My tears stopped. Fear subsided. My faith sustained me through working the twelve steps of AA in a way I never thought possible.

Most importantly, I found in the beginning paragraph of chapter five in *Alcoholics Anonymous: The Big Book* the formula for the truth.

Rarely have we seen a person fail who has thoroughly followed our path. Those who do not recover are people who cannot or will not completely give themselves to this simple program, usually men and women who are constitutionally incapable of being honest with themselves. There are such unfortunates. They are not at fault; they seem to have been born that way. They are naturally incapable of grasping and developing a manner of living which demands rigorous honesty. Their chances are less than average. There are those, too, who suffer from grave emotional and metal disorders, but many of them do recover if they have the capacity to be honest.
    —Alcoholic's Anonymous, page 58

When I first read these words, I no longer had to lie to cover my husband's drinking. I was married to an alcoholic, a good man with a bad disease. As at the beginning of an Al-Anon meeting, I now could say, "Hi, my name is Annetta and I am a grateful recovering family member." I felt different. Whole.

~~~~~

Jack began working for the Corson County Highway Department. He loved it. Although the disease was progressing and taking its toll on his work life, his job with the county afforded him a modicum of respect and responsibility. I was working for Mom and Dad.

Jack and I were living at the hotel, managing it for them. Leona, now widowed, had managed it previously. She was running for political office and no longer could do the day-to-day operation. She took an apartment upstairs. We lived in an apartment downstairs.

I continued to attend Al-Anon meetings. Jack hated it. I no longer cried when he lied, left us alone, or spent the money needed for basics on alcohol. I was working the twelve-step program, feeling more serene by knowing about the disease of alcoholism.

The relationship between Jack and Mom continued to deteriorate. One day, Jack decided it was time for us to build a house. He came home excited about finding a lot on which we could build. If we cleaned the lot of an old abandoned house ourselves, the cost would be minimal. "We can pour a basement, buy a premade house, and have it moved to the foundation," he said.

I was skeptical, but once again I was pregnant, trying to survive with two of the most significant people in my life drinking and caring for three small children. I was also cleaning the hotel, as well as cooking and serving three meals a day for our boarders. Now we were going to clear a lot and build a house. Great.

A man filling his coffee cup from Mom's massive, never-empty coffee pot held out his hand and said, "Hi, my name is Bob."

It was a stroke of luck. His office was located at the jail. By this time, my parents lived in the new country jail. Bob was an outreach counselor who provided chemical dependency services to county residents. I was cleaning and helping Mom at the jail, when Bob and I began to visit.

I told Bob that Al-Anon had saved my life. He invited me to come into his office and chat. He then changed my life.

"Annetta, who is the most important person in your life?" he asked.

Without hesitation, I responded, "My dad." Bob shook his head.

"Jack?" I responded. Same response.

"My children?" I offered. Again, his head went right to left. Now flustered, I asked, "Who is, then?"

He said, "What about you?" It was a watershed moment. He continued, "If you are not important to you, then how can you care for those you love?" It was as if I had stumbled across new-found information. Either that, or he was speaking a foreign language.

"Dad, please don't do it."

Amy, Emy, Jenny. I—very pregnant—was driving the pickup. Jack had said that he wanted treatment. As we drove toward the treatment center, he changed his mind and placed his hand on the door handle. He was going to jump from the moving vehicle.

"Dad, please don't do it."

Even in his intoxicated state, the plea from our eight-year-old daughter miraculously made his hand move from the door handle. The possibility and horror of their father jumping from the pickup made me physically sick. He entered treatment with intervention from an eight-year-old, six-year-old, and three-year-old.

Going into treatment and returning only to relapse became a common ritual with Jack. The relapses and progression of the disease brought more insanity. One time he ran from our bedroom to see if the pickup was parked in the driveway, admitting that the last he remembered was just leaving the bar in Morristown, seventeen miles from home. He had now progressed to bar drinking. At the time the worst road in the area lay between Morristown and our home. It was another miracle: no one was killed. A short time later, Jack's nephew was killed on the same stretch of road. Alcohol and denial were the causes.

The developing events brought more fear. My Al-Anon meetings helped to dissipate the pain, the fear. It was my daily spiritual intervention.

I decided to stage another intervention. Bob helped. This time, treatment was at Saint Joseph's Hospital. Gordie, amazing man, was Jack's counselor. Jack thrived. "I want to change," he told me, and, "I love you." My heart skipped.

He requested and received a weekend pass for a family wedding, his nephew's. I was nervous. Alcohol would be served. We made it through the wedding and then returned home to enjoy the rest of the evening. My little sister, Cece, babysat while we attended the wedding. The night was beautiful. In bed, I fell to a deep sleep. Excruciating pain woke me up.

"I'm hemorrhaging," I said softly to Jack. He jumped from bed. "What's wrong?" he asked as he pulled on his pants. We were in our seventh month of pregnancy.

"I don't know; it hurts." Picking up the phone, he dialed the hospital in Hettinger. He then ran to tell my little sister, who, thankfully, was staying overnight after staying with our children while we attended the family wedding.

"Cece," he said, "I am taking Annetta to the hospital."

"My Woman, My Woman, My Wife." The words of Marty Robbins's song played as we drove to the hospital. The pain was horrible, but it was the most intimate moment of our marriage. I knew that our baby and I were suspended between life and death. But my husband was sober, thanks to treatment. Even though he was driving, the baby and I were safe in his hands.

When we arrived at the hospital, the doctor yelled out questions: "How many pregnancies? Have you lost any family member?" The pain was excruciating. I could not remember. "I think someone died," I thought, but who?

My regular doctor was out of town grouse hunting. Thankfully, a surgeon was on call. Someone tried to call the local anesthesiologist. "Doctor," a nurse said, "the anesthesiologist is out of town." A sudden rush in the room. "Call…" The frantic tone of voice told me the situation. The hospital changed several requirements (standards) the night of our son's birth, including the ready availability of an anesthesiologist.

"She needs blood," I heard someone say.

"Jack and I have the same blood type," I heard myself respond. My husband was sober. He could provide blood for his wife and new baby. I asked for a priest. That night I had a cesarean birth—without medication. They later tried to explain the reason to me, something about how the lack of medication was due to the fact that, by the time they were able to take the baby, any anesthetic would make me have shallow breathing—or something like that. The explanation was unimportant. I had turned my baby's life and my own totally over to the hands of the men who had stood around the table, and I asked God to guide them.

I felt the incision on my stomach. I saw my son held over me, and then I was hit by the most unbearable physical pain. I felt a cry welling up from a deep source. I remember my mouth opening to release the depth of the pain, but nothing came out of my mouth. I entered another dimension.

A plane containing a medical staff from the University of Minnesota flew to the small airport in Hettinger. Our son, at a mere four pounds and one ounce, would require neonatal care not available anywhere near Hettinger. His weight fell to three pounds and fifteen and a half ounces.

I remember asking again for a priest. Father Dignan arrived to baptize our son. At that moment, I felt serenity. Nurses placed our son in a container that resembled a plastic coffin. I was only able to touch the top of his tiny head before very compassionate and professional men took our baby to the airport for the flight to the neonatal unit at the University of Minnesota.

We named him Chet Patrick.

As soon as I could walk, we flew to Minneapolis and I held my baby for the first time—with gloves, through a plastic case. A few hours later, the doctor told us of the miraculous turnaround of his blood gasses and other medical conditions. "It is a mother's touch, a mother's love that has turned him," he said. "How do you feel about him being returned to your local hospital earlier than we anticipated given what has occurred since your arrival?"

I was stunned. Our doctor had told me that he might have to stay up to a month, possibly longer, at the U. The next day, our son was brought back to our small town hospital. After getting the two girls in school, Jenny, a little over a year old, and I drove the one hundred forty miles to spend the day feeding and holding Chet, our new little family member. We returned by the time the other girls were home from school.

Very soon after, my doctor told me, "In my practice, there are two women who I would do this for." Then he broke the good news. "This child will do as well, if not better, at home with you." Again, I was stunned. Our doctor knew the situation. He also knew the overwhelming stress I was under. "Take Chet to the grocery store and weigh him. It is the most accurate scale in town. If he looses even an ounce, I want him returned." The only times I returned him to the doctor after that moment were for well-baby checkups.

Jack made it through the crisis, and then relapsed. The disease was progressing to a critical point. One night, I was nursing the baby, lying in our bed. Jack was gone, drinking. I heard the pickup motor in the driveway. I braced myself. After he stormed into the house, he pulled me from our bed. His fist landed in my mouth. He made me go to the kitchen. Our son began to cry. I held him close.

My face hurt. I felt blood coming from my mouth, welling up, creeping around my lips. Standing in our new, completed dream home, I held our infant son to my chest, tears streaming down my face.

"I am going to kill you," he slurred as he threw the bottle of catsup. I ducked. It missed my head—barely. The catsup splattered as it hit the wall behind me, a bright red stain marring the newly painted surface.

"Blow your head off."

He ranted as he fell toward the oak kitchen table. "Don't you think I know who you are?" he sneered. "You are a woman with a dead father and two dead sisters."

I tasted salt as my tears ran into my mouth. Tears. Fear. Numbness. I thought, "What has happened to my high-school sweetheart? My tender Jack? He drove through blizzards to spend an hour with me. Where did he go? He even stained the house rustic brown with gold trim. My favorite." My tears kept falling. Freshly baked caramel rolls cooled, resting on the counter in my spotless kitchen. They needed attention. So did my baby. I rocked him, back and forth, back and forth. He whimpered.

The baby's cry startled me back to reality. I comforted him. My thoughts seemed to drown in the tears that kept coming, but then resurfaced. I thought, "I married this man because he, like I, loved children. At their births, he held them in his strong arms and cried." That night, my baby's father was oblivious, living in a dark zone of intoxication, strong arms flailing.

I was scheduled to play the organ for Sunday Mass. A thought flashed through my mind: "How will I look in the morning? We cannot miss Mass. Do I have enough makeup to cover my face? Will the bruises show through?" Covering up the truth and the bruises had become a way of life. I was astute at the cover-up. Why had I stayed? The babies? Fear? Finances? Love? My own mother's retort? There were many reasons. No real answers. Yet.

Again, the baby's cry brought me to consciousness. He was our fourth child and at that time, our only son. I moved. I checked on our three beautiful, blond daughters, sleeping peacefully, snuggled safely in the freshly made beds, under sheets that smelled of clean air from drying on the clothes-line. Our three daughters were unaware of the nightmare that had played out in our kitchen and that would later play out in the bedroom.

Close by our lovely girls lay the dresses I had prepared for Sunday Mass; sweet little matching dresses, comfortable cotton, lavender and white. The girls' little white socks and newly polished shoes waited for them to awake Sunday morning. My tears fell on their bed. Thankfully, they were unaware.

Compared to other drinking nights, this was a good one. He finally passed out. Often the nightmare continued throughout the night. As a result, exhaustion was my constant companion. That night, my lip stung. The blood dried. I dried my tears. "Buck up," I told myself. No one needs to know. I kept smiling.

Sunday morning I dressed the children. The five of us walked to Saint Bonaventure, the church of my childhood, filled with hometown folks, including my parents and younger siblings. This Sunday morning was no different. Father Francis, the military veteran turned priest, smiled as we entered. I smiled and greeted him, my lip stinging, him not noticing.

I began to play the organ as Father and the altar boys lined for the processional preparing for Mass to begin. "Make me a channel of your peace," sang the congregation as my fingers moved across the white keys. The children sat still. Amy, our oldest, held the baby. No one knew of the cover-up, common in an alcoholic home. The makeup had worked. It always did. Always.

I had discovered I was pregnant again. Our fifth child. Natural family planning was not working, not in an alcoholic marriage.

The disease progressed. I decided one more time. Treatment. This time at Heartview in Mandan, North Dakota. It was during the week the patient's family spent time in the same treatment center learning about the disease of alcoholism and the impact on the family called Family Week that I told Jack, "I will no longer continue to allow our family to implode. No matter how much I love you. The children need sanity, safety. I will no longer allow you to destroy the entire family. I will not bring another child into this chaos."

When I learned I was pregnant for the fifth time, I was already experiencing complications, and my doctor told me that he wanted to do ultrasounds three times over a span of a couple of weeks. If there were no audible heartbeats, we would have to make a decision.

After the appointment when he told me this, I walked out on the steps of the clinic. I was bombarded by a cacophony of emotions: overwhelming fear and sadness, as well as a consciousness of the fact that, at that moment, other than feeling the presence of God, I felt alone. Jack was in the throws of alcoholism. He was meting out violence against me on a whim. We had no health insurance. I would face another C-section. The doctor did not know if I would live through another pregnancy. And other than calling on my baby sister, I couldn't depend on family for support.

Mom's distance continued. Dad, too, was absent, telling me later he felt helpless until I was ready to make a decision. One of my siblings shared the feelings permeating through my family upon learning of my fifth pregnancy. "Are you trying to kill yourself?" the sibling asked. No, but I was in an intolerable situation; I felt I had nowhere to go. I needed— wanted—love, support. Instead, I felt distance, criticism.

Questions raced through my head: "What will happen to my five babies if I do not live?" Then I thought, "This is the kind of situation in which women seek abortions." I abhorred abortion. And up to that point, I had been judgmental of women even considering it. But I suddenly understood the implications of how and why, the reality of it all.

Abortion is grim; no woman would have one if her alternatives did not appear more forbidding. Yet when will the church and society ask, "What is the reason any woman would seek an abortion? How do we treat women? Children? Where are we when women are in crisis? Do we offer the support they need?"

It was another watershed moment. I was judgmental. All those questions were formidable.

I made a vow. Never, and I meant never, would I—could I—judge any woman in a similar position. However, I would and could walk with them through their pain, supporting, loving, and providing.

"You will have to have a cesarean," my doctor confirmed. My doctor and I had been through significant life-and-death perils in the creation of my family. He was aware of the reality of the alcoholism and abuse, and now, another pregnancy. He knew what that could mean to my physical and psychological well-being.

Our Dr. Bob, God, and I brought Bret Joseph to the world. Jack, in the full grips of alcoholism, was present when Bret was born. I had known for some time that our marriage was over, yet I remained in it until after the birth, so our baby would know his father was present. I hadn't wanted Bret to lack a father at that moment, although Jack had not been there during the pregnancy, it was not for lack of love for Bret, but for a lack of love for himself.

And Bret somehow knew, from the moment of his birth, that his mom needed a break.

He grew into a tender child, a loving son and brother. He became for his sisters and brother a source of great joy. As a boy, his was a positive personality, filled with energy. His interactions with his older brother, usually flavored with a twist of mischievousness, reminded me of the planning Vonnie and I had done. As little people, Chet and Bret were inseparable. The two boys, younger than their sisters, thought that protecting their big sisters from suitors was their responsibility. Any boy who dated their sisters went through hell. The ones who stayed and married their sisters were the survivors.

When I was pregnant with Bret, Mary the mother of God was my constant companion. I was pregnant and alone. Afraid. Jack was always gone, drinking. I visualized Mary sitting on the side of my bed. We had conversations, prayed together. She gave me strength to keep going, humor to laugh at the mundane and even at the pain and loneliness. During our conversations, I experienced Mary as the suffering servant, the face of God in the Holy Family. She was real, no longer a plaster-of-paris statue.

She had been in a real, blended family, struggling, loving together. I knew Jesus had to have worn diapers. As a young person, Jesus went to the temple to teach without parental permission. Jesus today would probably be called a problem child. Today the world would probably call his family dysfunctional. I felt as though I were in good company. The Holy Family: blended, rejected, and at times afraid. But they kept going. Father Peyton's words kept coming back to me: "The family that prays together, stays together."

Jack refused to attend church and pray with us as a family. He disappeared when I was teaching the children their prayers, "Angel of God," "Hail Mary," "Our Father." His conversion to the faith was short-lived after marriage. Drinking became more important than going to church or praying.

"As long as you keep letting him beat you, you are spitting in the face of God," Father Francis pleaded as he continued to direct me, the one who felt directionless. This meeting followed another week of Jack's absence, of not knowing if Jack were dead or alive. "What if he's killed himself?" I asked Father. "He threatened." I began to weep, choking back the fear of the thought that the father of my children may have ended his life.

The military man made priest roared back, "If he does and you feel one ounce of guilt, I will personally kick you in the ass." The strength of his words stopped the tears. I had no doubt Father met what he said. He was correct; the body is the vessel that holds the soul, the spirit. No one deserves abuse. No one.

"That's a bunch of shit," was Jack's response after four treatments for alcoholism. I looked long and hard at the father of my children, my high-school sweetheart, and my husband. I had just returned from the hospital after giving birth. I gently lifted Bret Joseph, our youngest, from the bassinet, as the other four stood around me, smiling with their beautiful blue eyes. Jack refused to follow the recommendations of the treatment center. No recovery for him. And no amount of pleas or tears could change his mind.

When I said, "Enough. Leave," he did. When the six of us walked out to our newly planted yard and I felt the summer breeze, I felt free, liberated. I painted the new house my favorite color: soft green. The same color as my bridesmaids' dresses. As I painted, the children played, chirping, laughing, safe from chaos.

Through prayer, courage, Al-Anon, Ruth, Father Francis, and, yes, Mom, the time of decision presented itself. I filed for divorce. Jack continued to drink. I had Mom's total support. It felt different.

Jack spent time incarcerated. The disease took him from chief of police to incarceration. Jack was no criminal. When in the disease, he acted irresponsibly, as do most alcoholics. He remarried.

His second wife called and asked, "What do I do?"

"Get him to a detox, then treatment," I advised.

His brother called. Same question. Same answer.

His second marriage did not last. It took the loss of two families, incarceration, a stroke, and paralysis to stop the disease. During our years together, he had refused to read *Alcoholics Anonymous* or to attend AA. He refused a simple program with a simple solution.

Our marriage possessed moments of shear joy. Fighting was not an option that either of us ever needed or wanted. Our relationship was loving, gentle, peaceful. Until alcohol entered. The disease of alcoholism ravaged my dream. "Jack, I feel like you are drowning and I can't swim," I often said. The disease took my husband and my children's father. I felt helpless. In reality, I was.

I married Jack because he wore wing tip shoes and loved spinach. He also loved children. And they loved him. I wanted a house filled with a husband who loved me and his children. The disease took the husband and the father. The dream of a home filled with children remained. I never took it for granted.

Early in my motherhood, one Mother's Day, Jack bought me a mother's ring. Two stones: one for Amy and one for Emy. I filled in the other three as babies arrived and the disease took him. I wear it every day. He gave me a ring, made me a mother. I am eternally grateful. He gave me such a striking, sturdy family. I never, not once, reviled the man who helped create such gifts, my experiences of the Divine, my glimpses of God at their births. I will always love the person who helped create such gifts.

"Don't cry because it's over. Smile because it happened," I said more than once when I looked at the five beautiful faces of my children.

Chapter 13

My life as a single parent began. Maintaining normalcy was among my most important responsibilities. One yearly event—a highlight in our hometown—brought normalcy: Santa Claus Day. Santa Claus was any man the organizers could find to do the job. Some years a skinny Santa showed up; other years, the flesh popped out all over, and alcohol lingered on Santa's breath.

One particular year, the powers that be decided to bring Santa in on a snowmobile. It was not good. My children were small; the fat man in a red suit had a young Mrs. Claus with him. She had beautiful long red hair. Santa Claus, with Mrs. Santa holding his belt, soared down our main street on what would be a fateful snowmobile ride.

Excitement grew among the waiting children. My own children were flush with anticipation. My throat began to tighten when, realizing that something was off, I thought, "I don't think Santa knows how to drive that machine." Wham. They slammed right into the side of the Legion Hall.

Emy looked up at me, unmoved by the fact that Santa had had an accident. She just looked disappointed. "Mom, that's not Santa. That's Uncle Joe." Whoever had put Joe, my baby brother, behind the handles of a snowmobile needed an intelligence test. Anyone in his right mind—including pretty Mrs. Claus—should have known that he had no clue about machines.

A divorced, single woman, I learned, becomes open to the ugly side of humanity. Called "grass widows" and other demeaning names, divorced women were treated like fifth-class citizens. At that time in history, divorced people, especially women, knew they did not fit in any class of society. I realized it quickly.

I realized a few other things. First, married women protected their husbands as if to fear the divorced woman would take their husband away from them. It was a realization I never knew until I became divorced. Therefore, I devised my own strategy. When meeting a couple, I learned early on to always acknowledge the wife first, and then speak to the husband. Second, I found out that I was looked at as a kind of bait, and the crows began to circle. A local man came to our door bearing licorice. Let's just say he was no Harry Kittelson bearing bubble gum. The kids nicknamed him the Licorice Man. He was not invited back.

Another significant event occurred and changed my reality. I felt his hand on my arm. He swung me around, grabbed me, and planted a kiss on my lips. I felt nauseous. The smell of alcohol and perspiration saturated the experience. I was repulsed, confused. "What?" I physically jumped back from him. Immediately I began to question myself asking myself did I do something to cause this? Was I too nice to him? I had just accepted a pastoral position from this man. For the next few months, I did what I had to do to extricate myself

from the situation. He was a priest. The experience opened
a door to a dark side within my church life and experience
that I never knew existed. It involved abuse on several lev-
els. Later, a wise sensitve, pastoral bishop, a gentle priest
and my spiritual director named what this man did to me.
They helped me sort through the feelings, the reality. The
abuse. This man showed up a couple more times in my life.
However, by that time, I had found my voice and although,
he continued to smell of perspiration and alcohol, I con-
fronted him. He did not accept responsibility. My faith did
not change. But my reality did. His presence marks a dark
moment on my faith journey. I kept going.

I later wrote a monthly social justice column. One column was about the nuances of the so called liberal "pro-
choice" and so called conservative "pro-life" positions in the
abortion debate. In it, I stated that, personally, I had never
met a person who actually believed anything positive about
abortion and how politicians use the topic to either win votes
or berate their opponent. Yet, the same person will vote
against any care for a child after it is born including health
care and education. I also wrote that I had, however, come
across many who feel strongly that decisions made around
reproduction should be about the woman making the decision, with the help of her doctor, clergyperson, spouse, and
loved ones. Our responsibility is to love and offer support to
the woman through these difficult times.

After the article came out, I received a phone call from
the priest who smelled of alcohol and perspiration ada-
mantly accusing me of being pro-abortion. I listened. He
missed the entire point of the column. After finishing his
monologue, I asked, "If the women you have been involved

with were to have become pregnant, would you have been there during the pregnancy, birth, and life of the child providing financially, emotionally, educationally, and spiritually?" The phone went dead. He knew that I knew that he knew. Knowing this man's predilection to spread untruths, I wasn't sure what he was going to do, or what kind of trouble may occur. Months later he called. I received an apology.

~

When I entered single parenthood alone, kneeling, praying before Mass, I talked to God about my fear. Paralyzing fear. I asked, "How am I going to provide alone for the five children?" Deep in prayer, I looked up. There he was. A statue. Joseph, with his gentle smile, holding baby Jesus. "What the heck, it's worth a try," I thought. Leaving Mass, I announced to the five chicklets, "I found us a dad."

Five voices asked in unison, "Who?"

"Saint Joseph," I announced. "If he could shepherd the Savior of the world, he should be able to help me raise you." They weren't impressed. But from that day forward, we prayed to him at every meal. Today, they continue the prayer with their families. Saint Joseph was the one constant we had when they went through Catholic grade and high school. Joseph was my solace in moments of panic. I talked to him. I felt comfort.

Saint Joseph our family patron. I still have a small Saint Joseph statue from that time that I keep in the kitchen. His head has been superglued to his body more than once. Gentle Saint Joseph made a difference.

~

"How are we going to buy groceries, pay the house payment?"

During this time, my canning of meats, as well as vegetables from the garden, kept us filled. Shortly after I filed the divorce papers, I walked up the steps of the courthouse, crying with each step. Jack did not pay child support. I didn't expect it. The point was mute. Even caring for himself, in his state, was impossible. How would he care for his family?

I entered the office of Aid for Dependent Children. It was the most humiliating moment of my life and one of the most significant. Humiliation brought humility. My motivation was my children. That moment I made a vow: I will become a taxpayer and help others in the same situation. And I did.

Poverty suffocates. Homelessness does, too, especially with five children. Fear becomes your companion. I learned this the hard way. A personal way.

I was offered a job working seven days a week, on call, at a rural parish with a boarding school with international students, one of whom lived with us, when we were forced to move. The parish priest had hired me and suddenly left the parish. He had notified the bishop in writing.

My children and I were left to pick up the pieces, especially with respect to the students whom he had brought from Honduras and Ethiopia. The pastor and I had been the only real support system they had had in the United States.

I was already exhausted from raising my family and working at the parish and school. Then the priest told me he was resigning, and that my family and I needed to leave. Father told me that we had to find housing. This was not the first time my family had faced homelessness. We had lost our home right after Jack left.

I had no choice but to jump in my station wagon and drive the fifty miles to the nearest town to try and find a home.

We had no money. I would have to rely on assistance. I looked at two apartments. Two apartment managers gave me positive responses. I was deeply relieved. I went back to pack my family.

Father left on a Sunday afternoon. On Monday, I was notified by one of the apartment owners that I wouldn't be able to rent from him after all: I had too many children. So I jumped into the car and rushed back over those fifty miles to confirm in person with the second manager of the other apartment building.

He answered the door, and said, "I liked you, but the owner has said that you have too many children."

I stood on the stoop of the apartment house. Tears surfaced. "Okay, God and Joseph, I need help," I said to myself as I turned to leave. After driving to the Donut Hole for coffee and a moment of peace, I opened the newspaper to the apartment section. I found a potential lead. I mentally noted that I wouldn't tell the manager about the five little people who would be living in the apartment with me. I would just bring them in one at a time.

But when I got in front of her, I decided against dishonesty. I told the truth. She looked at me, excited. "I will call the owner. I will let you know," she said. To my surprise, sight unseen, the owner, Bill Bianco, said, "Give this woman and her children a place to live." From a perspective of faith, this man surely lived his baptism. In many ways, he changed our lives.

"Poverty will not define you," I told my children. "It will provide you with a different way to approach life. Be better, not bitter," I went on to say. "No cynicism; only gratitude allowed."

~

"You can do it," she said in her soft, gentle way.

"Sister, I have no money. I have five babies. But I also have a desire to graduate with a degree."

She said it again. "You can do it."

I had made a visit to Mary College before. That trip had been ten years earlier with my father, prior to my attending Presentation College, Karren's death, my marriage to Jack, giving birth five times. The earlier trip to Mary College Dad had liked it. So had I, but for some reason, I decided to attend Presentation College.

Sister Mary Walker. Benedictine. She was the gentle soul with the gentle voice who provided the support I needed at a very fearful time in my life. I kept her voice and words in my mind as I worked every night after the children fell asleep. With my baby son beside me, I read books to keep my mind fresh. I attended any class available in our rural area, and then we made the big move.

Mom questioned the move. Dad was silent.

"Mom, isn't it exciting we are all going to school at the same time?" Amy asked with a sparkle in her beautiful eyes. After they were in school, I went to classes, making it home before their school bus pulled up. I fed them a snack. Then homework, dinner, pajamas, and bed for the children, and studying for Mom until the early hours. I'd sleep a couple of hours and be off on the same schedule. It stayed that way until the day I walked across the graduation stage at the University of Mary and my children yelled "Yea, Mom!" as I was handed my bachelor of arts degree.

We had just accomplished a four-year degree in two years and made the dean's list in the midst of a twenty-two hour semester. We worked hard and celebrated everything. Sister Mary Walker, provided instruction in several of my theology classes. The gentle-voiced woman who said I could do it helped me accomplish it. Her own life was not easy. She gave us her heart, exquisite mind, and pastoral gifts, with profound effects.

"They came from distant lands to homestead on the prairie," I read and reflected. I was sitting on a bench under the beautiful sculpture of The Pioneer Family, placed appropriately on the grounds of the North Dakota State Capitol. While most people saw the lush green lawn of the capitol grounds, the deco-style building built from materials during World War II, completed in 1934, in the depths of the Great Depression, I watched another pioneer family, genetically tied to those early immigrants.

I watched my children, small blond wonders, romping and playing. "This is our playground," I told them. This wonderful place became our playground. The pool in front of the the Heritage Center on the capitol grounds was full of water, and we thought of it as our family wading pool. I watched the five towheads running and laughing as I leaned against the Heritage Center building, lovingly, proudly watching the beauty of my children.

Visitors to the grounds would exclaim, "Whose children are they?" I would respond with satisfaction, "Aren't they gorgeous?" We had no money to pay for the local swimming pool or YMCA. Parks and playgrounds were our sources of wonder. However, for them I made the capitol grounds special.

We were a unique pioneer family—a pioneer family in the late 1970s. Single-parent families were wholly uncommon at that time and in that place. When my children attended school, most kids had two parents. The parenting wasn't perfect, but nevertheless, there were usually two parents at home. My children were looked upon as different. I did not want their circumstances to deter them. I wanted them to take a unique route, to see things differently.

He ran from the bus, his little body quivering. When he got in the apartment, he put his back against the door. "What's wrong?" I gasped as I placed my arms around my seven-year-old son, my oldest boy, who resembled little Rick Schroder in *The Champ*, tears welling in his big blue eyes.

"Mom, teacher made fun of my gloves." It was not the first time cruel things had been said to one of my children. My children were not invited into some people's homes because we were a single-parent family; we were told as much. I could feel my heart break. "She isn't as fortunate as we are," I told my son. "She has two matching gloves. You have two colors, she has only one." His tears dried. He smiled. I prayed for the teacher who was ignorant of what it can mean to live in poverty. Later, she apologized.

We learned to celebrate the small things. If someone was struggling with something and the situation improved, we celebrated. I'd make popcorn. If we had butter, I melted it and put it on the popcorn. No matter what, we celebrated. Bumps were certainly scattered across our paths, but we overcame them. And we celebrated and kept going.

Life presents challenges. Challenges present possibilities. George Bernard Shaw once said, "Some people look at things and say 'Why?' I dream of things that never were and say 'Why not?'" This became my mantra. I believed in the possibilities. I was not going to let our circumstances destroy us. When we were denied housing, I told my children "We are financially poor millionaires. We have what many people don't have. Even during the most difficult times, we have love in every corner of our home." They responded with smiles.

"Mom, can we go to McDonald's?"

I replied, "If we can find thirty-seven cents." Into the car seat their little hands would go.

"I found a penny."

"Here's a dime."

"Mom, I found a quarter."

"We're still short," I said. More hands. More squeals. Another dime. We had it. "Okay. We have enough." The old, gold, heavy station wagon filled with kids and groceries, paid for with our blessed food stamps from the grocery warehouse we pulled into the parking lot. I entered the McDonald's. "One hamburger, please."

"That will be thirty seven cents," the boy behind the counter said, handing me the bag containing the precious burger.

"Thank you," I said. Returning to the station wagon, I took out the hamburger, all five pairs of eyes resting on it. On the first round, everyone took one bite. Six. One more time around. Six more bites. Most people never count the bites when they eat a McDonald's hamburger. My kids did. Everyone had two bites. It was a good day.

Even when things were tough for us, Christmas held special meaning. After Jack left, the children chose what we'd have for Christmas Eve dinner. "Steak!" was always the resounding answer. Every year. Steak was a delicacy in our home. I could scrape together enough for two steaks if I saved pennies over a span of time.

The Jaycee's provided for more than one Christmas at our house. The parish once brought a box with a turkey and all the fixings. The providers always showed up. Most of the time we never knew their names. Yet my gratitude went out to them without bounds. It still does.

⁓

At night, I would cry. Prayers to keep me going. Prayers asking that my babies would be kept safe. Prayers. Prayers. Prayers. And pinching every penny. And reading my Al-Anon book. If I had enough gas in the car, I attended Al-Anon meetings.

⁓

In 1984, the children and I received my bachelor's degree in ministry and addiction counseling from the University of Mary, the same school Dad and I had visited after my high-school graduation.

And ten years after that, the university invited Mom and Dad to attend the alumni awards ceremony; I was to be honored. That night, Dad handed me flowers before I received the alumni award from the University of Mary. His eyes watered. So did mine.

Chapter 14

"We'd like you to interview," the voice on the other end of the line said. The call had come from the diocese.

After graduating from the University of Mary, I began to seek employment. I had sent in three applications: one to a treatment center, the second to a school for a counseling position, and the third to the diocese for a position working for the new bishop who had been installed the previous year. This call gave me my first opportunity to practice interviewing. At least so I thought—until I met the bishop.

This diocese, the "see" or seat of the local bishop, covered a large area of real estate in the Midwest. My involvement at the diocesan level started a few years earlier. I was volunteering at a rural Catholic high school, developing and executing a youth program. I invited the then-bishop to be the speaker at our culminating yearly event, something we called "Mom's My Mate and Dad's My Date," a dinner and dance. The family theme included a speech given by the diocesan bishop.

Inviting him assured the attendance of uninvolved parents. Church and work, in that particular parish, came before marriages and children. Work was everything. For some, alcohol ranked third; for many, it ranked first. Children, in more homes than I care to admit, ranked behind the farm animals. These parents would come for the bishop, not specifically for their children. Thus, this bishop, while not a pastoral or warm individual, was my calling card to nonparticipating parents.

The family was to be the topic of his speech. Instead, this man took the opportunity to speak about divorce and the negative impact divorced people had on the church. Sitting in the chair next to the lectern, I listened as the bishop spoke judgmentally and critically about the divorced. From my vantage point, I saw the people sitting casually in their chairs become uncomfortable as the bishop essentially ranted.

He showed no sensitivity, no grasp of the reality or reason Catholic people might find themselves in the throws of a divorce. No forgiveness. None. I realized at that moment that the only two people in the gymnasium with any modicum of ease were the bishop and me. He was clueless. I was not.

Visiting with the parish priest following the event, the bishop asked about me, unaware that I was one of the horrible people he had just described. "Where did she come from?" he asked, adding, "How did the parish find a person who is so spiritually positive? So Catholic?"

My pastor saw the Bishop's compliment as a convenient entrance to the truth. He said, "She shares a refreshing level of commitment and does so with a deep, healthy faith."

The bishop continued, unabated, saying, "She mentioned she has five children. What does her husband do?"

Father replied, "She is divorced." The priest had taken full advantage of this teachable moment. When Father retold the story to me, I smiled. So did he.

Skidding, I heard the gravel thrown up against the car as I pressed the break. My beat-up Chevy had missed the turn in front of the chancery, the bishop's residence. It would be my first meeting with him after being named to the bishop's cabinet. At that time, I would be the only woman.

I was late. Jane, the bishop's secretary, greeted me with a knowing smile. She nodded and pointed me to the large conference dining room. Rushing by the rich wood and stark beauty of the deco-style building, I realized the significance of the moment. Our family journey was worth this moment. I had arrived. I thus began the next two decades of being Catholic.

Hired to be the director of the program serving separated, divorced, and widowed Catholics, I began my employment with the diocese in 1984, completing two search-committee interviews, an interview with the new bishop, and an offer a day later by the bishop himself. What I thought would be a practice interview was my one and only interview with him. I said yes to the offer. With what I soon learned was his characteristic compassion, he invited me to begin a month after the children began school and when I had "recovered" from a rigorous clinical pastoral education internship.

On October 1, 1984, I began a nineteen-year journey walking with the people of the diocese. Working with, and for, two bishops, and witnessing the reform in the church ushered in by Pope John XXIII and Vatican II. Prior to Vatican II, divorced Catholics were the bane of the church. Like the F- word, the word "divorce" was considered filthy. Anyone who found himself or herself in the position was treated similarly.

Furthermore, people stayed in abusive, sometimes fatal, marriages from fear of condemning their immortal souls, were they to leave their marriages. I know; I was one of those people. My faith, my church, and my family were my life. To leave it, in my eyes and the eyes of most Catholics at that time, meant being ostracized from the sacramental life of the church.

In my case, Father Francis, a Benedictine, my parish priest, saved my life and the lives of my children when he encouraged me to leave the abusive marriage and begin the annulment process. Without his support and the courage I found in Al-Anon, only God knows the catastrophic results that would have unfolded in our home.

Vatican II brought a new energy, a new understanding, a new spirit to the church. Prior to Vatican II, the church was repressive, suppressive, obsessive, depressive. Vatican II taught a new understanding of God: the fear-based regulator in heaven no longer existed. It never had. This was a new concept for most Catholics. God, we were now taught about a God of compassion, mercy, and justice, not of wrath and judgment. In reality, Vatican II, although seemingly introducing "new" ideas, was a return to ideas of early church. In many ways, we were turning back to the basics, to the church instituted by Christ in his early ministry. We rediscovered Catholicism.

Our new bishop hired me. He was completely different from his predecessor, with a different personality and style. He was a visionary, pastorally sensitive and just, supportive of new ideas and possibilities. Politically, his intelligent and compassionate work to advance justice, as well as his pastoral sensitivity, came at great cost. He never received the red hat.

Until this man walked through the doors of the chancery, treatment for addiction or sexual or moral struggles received the kind of judgment, criticism, or denial I heard the previous bishop give the night of the Mom's My Mate and Dad's My Date dinner. And prior to this man's arrival, any real issue in the diocese was denied, the offender quietly removed, or the person reporting the situation told to pray for his or her own soul. Ignorance was bliss.

It was obvious to me that, in our diocese, alienated, divorced Catholics were straying away from the church in record numbers. I also recognized how the divorced, alcoholic Catholic suffered a double blow. And many others, not just the divorcees or the addicted, felt alienated. Even though women filled most of the pews in every Catholic community, no women appeared on the altar. Even the *thought* of female altar servers had not entered the consciousness of most Catholics. And although women provided most of the education, health care, and sacristy care at that time, they were not recognized for their mission or ministry in the same ways as priests were.

So as professional layperson (someone who works in the church and who has been baptized but not ordained or from a religious order), and specifically as a woman, I was remarkable. Miraculous, even. With that knowledge, and as an annulled, educated Catholic professional woman, I began walking the mission of teaching a dubious people what a ministry focused on divorced people could entail.

Divorced Catholics. Once a blight on the church. Now they had a ferocious advocate, as did those suffering from the disease of alcoholism. My outreach to the alienated and suffering began on the first day of my employ. Because the bishop supported me, I was able to take risks. The signature scripture for the office was the Bible passage about the divorced woman at the well. With his characteristic compassion, Jesus had revealed his public ministry to a divorced woman.

Early in my work, I found that there was a lack of education around annulments, both concerning the historical context and the purpose of the process. A marriage is annulled when an appropriate authority determines that the sacramental bond never took place, often due to circumstances beyond the control of one or both parties. This misconception included the idea that you could buy an annulment and the idea that the church practiced favoritism in the granting of annulments. Neither were true.

Presenting annulment as an opportunity to experience the healing love of Christ, as well as to heal, forgive, and love, was foreign to most people. And the opportunity for healing was needed. "People do not get married to get divorced," I said, "especially Catholic people." For some, there is no greater pain than to become a divorced person. When one is a Catholic, this can be especially true. Of course, alcoholism can undermine any marriage, Catholic or not. The ramifications of alcoholism often forge the foundation to divorce.

I love priests. I've worked with over a hundred. The men who have worn the collar that have made up this cast of characters have influenced my life in ways I cannot express. They've had diverse personalities, strengths, and weaknesses. All have influenced my spiritual journey. Some forced me to ask the questions. Others, I questioned. Some of the priests offered excellent pastoral care; others were less able. In my new position, I was about to begin working with the fullest cast yet.

Religious, diocesan, and incardinated priests provided religious leadership in our diocese. Religious priests lived in the community and sometimes worked in parishes, adhering to the commitment of their religious vows of poverty, chastity, and obedience. Diocesan priests, ordained by and obedient to the bishop, were my most common ministry colleagues. The incardinated came from other dioceses for a myriad of reasons. Some sent out of a questioning situation, but most were sent due to priestly commitment.

In our diocese, there were three Benedictine religious communities: one men's abbey and two women's monasteries. All three influenced thousands of people over the years. The abbey, with its cattle ranch, was involved in printing and in running a boy's high school. The monks had brilliant minds and great pastoral gifts. The men of Richardton Abbey and those who resided there I hold close to my heart.

The women of Sacred Heart and Annunciation monasteries built hospitals, schools, and nursing homes. They taught and worked in parishes, nurturing the faith through prayer, work, and care. And the sisters lived the motto of the Benedictine's "Let all be received as Christ."

The priests in my life were complex. Some were pure and without guile; they were, and are, saints. They took the ordinary and made it holy. They were so easy to love. Some were a combination of light and dark. These were the ones with whom I often struggled, yet they taught me the spiritual principles of patience, understanding, compassion, and sometimes confrontation.

"Although you're a woman, since you work for the bishop, I won't make you come early and make dinner for the priests," said the host priest of the deanery meeting at which I was to speak.

He wasn't joking. Not this man. He was perhaps the most sexist human being on the planet. He felt most comfortable on a pedestal. I know. I worked under him, and he often reminded that he was the boss and that any woman, including me, was best fit to cook, clean, and provide for his every need.

This time it was different. He was no longer dealing with a submissive underling. I had found my voice. And with the support and encouragement of the bishop, I was helping others to find theirs.

I was not, and never will be, an ardent feminist. However, I do know—and the nuns taught us girls this—that women are intelligent, verbal, and talented. We must use our abilities. The women's movement addressed social, economic, and political issues, as Jesus had, encouraging women to speak out. But for too long, in the course of trying to please, I had not used my voice. I was ready to that night.

Perhaps my conviction stemmed from having been abused by a man who happened to wear the collar, having finally received my bachelor's degree, or having dealt with an alcoholic husband in the throws of an attempt to destroy me. Perhaps it was all that and more. I said, "Father, I am speaking tonight. If you like, tonight as host, you will have the opportunity to serve all of your guests, including me." He never made another sexist remark within my earshot again.

Sexism is a primal sin. Yet, men and society still use it to "put women in their place." Sometimes subtly. Other times, not. Fortunately, the two bishops I worked with lived the gospel of justice that Jesus taught, especially when it came to women.

Those who take advantage of power often do so to cover up inadequacies of the ego or to bolster a weak or threatened sense of self. In nearly any situation, an inflated ego is a nightmare. More than one priest I encountered came with an inflated ego. A wise bishop once said of one such pastor, "Oh, Annetta; he is not a pastor to the people. They are pastors to him."

The priests of my childhood and young adulthood formed my faith, guided me in life decisions. Some I listened to. Others I did not. I often found their advice sound. Often, I paid a heavy price for failing to heed their wisdom.

———

"I have no idea who . . . I don't know . . . It did not occur," said Cardinal Joseph Bernadine while standing in front of a mass of microphones. He was my role model, my mentor of pastoral care. This man stood with dignity and in pain. A beloved, respected priest, a cardinal, was responding to accusations of sexual abuse. How did it come to this?

———

Prior to the Cardinal Bernadine standing in front of a microphone, I received a call from one of the priests in our diocese. "Will you talk to a young woman who came to my office with her mother?" he asked me with a sense of sadness. He explained what he knew of the situation.

The young women had told him that, as a teenager, a well-known priest had continuously touched her sexually. She, the first of many victims with whom I worked, eventually told her mother about it when she reached adulthood. They told their trusted parish priest.

"Will you talk to her?" he asked me. Without hesitation, I said yes, and I met with the young woman. I called the bishop. He responded immediately to the victim. He also immediately addressed the perpetrator. This occurred in the first few months of my work in the diocese.

Victim after victim came through the door of my office. They trusted me. So did the perpetrators. The sexual-abuse scandal occurred in our church and society long before Jeff Anderson, the famed (by some, infamous) Minneapolis attorney brought it to the light of day. Even as the first few victims came to see me, I knew that this was going to be difficult and big. It wasn't a matter of if, but of when.

I treated the victims who came forward with compassionate care. So did the bishop. Tears of compassion shared. They wanted to be validated in their pain. They were. Their stories revealed many different truths about the perpetrators. I then discovered that some of those perpetrators had been victims themselves. Some had been sexually abused as children, thinking it their fault, and had joined the priesthood to cleanse the shame and pain.

Others, those who were psychosexually underdeveloped, had come into their adolescent sexual awakening late, in adulthood, after ordination. Sometimes this was due to the fact that seminaries taught any sexual awakening as temptation of the flesh, and sinful. Priests, both those in training and those who were ordained, were not encouraged do discuss any sexual struggles.

Of the cases with which I was involved, the most difficult to witness were those involving priests who consciously made a decision to abuse another person and who chose to use their authority to do it. I did not experience many such cases, but when I did, I felt that the perpetrators deserved prison.

In my eyes, among the heartbreaking travesties were the cases of those priests who had been falsely accused. Cardinal Joseph Bernadine was one such priest. Falsely accused. Their good names were never restored and for some the experience was devastating. I knew more than one healthy priest who, after the false accusation, died of illnesses not present before the accusation. They deserved compassion and in many ways are modern-day saints: good men brutalized and marginalized by the abuse scandal.

Then there were those who abused, but were never questioned.

More than once in my work during this difficult time, I dealt with a conartist who entered my office with dark intentions. And more than once, I'm sorry to say, I was taken. Their intention was to swindle and defraud, and they succeeded. While I listened compassionately, unaware of their real motives, psychological illnesses, or addiction, they took, criminally. Some used the sex abuse scandal to do so.

While the scandal fueled the disdain of those inclined toward anti-Catholicism, it also painfully seared the hearts of faithful Catholics. There is no ambiguity about this. The grief felt by Catholics in parish pews was intense. The grief was palpable. This fact seems to have been largely ignored. But the church is a community. When one in the community suffers, we all suffer.

The community continues to suffer. Large sums of money have been paid out. Programs have been destroyed. Well-educated, intelligent, faithful, committed professionals have lost their jobs due to lack of funds. The list goes on.

Any type of abuse devastates the soul as well as the body. Sexual trauma in particular enters the depth of the soul. We are created as sexual beings, and so sexual trauma impacts our very core.

Sexual trauma is not a recent phenomenon, but rather is

as old as humanity. In my professional life, I have witnessed it all. In one area in which I worked, generational incest was so common they thought it was normal. Also common in that world were the resulting pregnancies and back-alley abortions. I secured the strength of a pastoral priest to help me help these families.

Significant studies show that there are a myriad of causes of sexual violations such as incest, including generations of sexual, physical, and emotional abuse. And the solution is not to deny our sexuality. We know we are sexual. Every cell of our body provides that vessel of sexuality. God created every human person sexual. But as sexual beings, we are to rejoice in the gift, not demean, abuse, or use it in a way to destroy another.

I believe that we are meant to celebrate, love, and enjoy our sexuality. In our tradition, we believe the body contains the spirit. God's spirit. When we truly believe it, we care for it. Unfortunately, most human beings are not taught to love themselves as the gifts that they are. Luckily, I was taught this from a priest. Once, sometime after I had been married, I confessed to a priest that I had enjoyed the gifts of the body and that I felt that doing so must be a sin. This wise man told me, "God created the body to be celebrated. One of the greatest prayers, if not the greatest, is when two people who in commitment, fidelity love, respect, and honor one another enjoy their bodies. And yes, in the intimacy both people are to be treated with dignity." In the Catholic Church, we call this the sacrament of marriage. This is a teaching I pass on every day in my professional and private life.

Unfortunately this priest was the exception. Sex is the greatest issue the church must deal with today. It encompasses birth control, abortion, sexual orientation, treatment of women, and celibacy. Failing to address these issues in a healthy way fuels sexual and emotional abuse, domestic violence, chemical dependency, homelessness, poverty, and the maltreatment of women—literally all of the social ills. Yet, we are not dealing with it gracefully.

Until the issue became one of money, it stayed in the closet. In the throes of the abuse scandal, one bishop I know once invited others to the microphone to share their pain, their hurt, and the impact of the clergy sexual abuse on their faith. He was the exception. "Do not mention the 's' word," one school principle said to me just before I was to present to an entire high school. Following the presentation, I was surrounded by teenagers asking me questions about the "s" word, about sexuality and living life as sexual beings.

Sex, and all the topics related to it, remain taboo. The sex abuse scandal has only fortified this silence, when it really has been an opportunity for the church to transform itself. Destructive although it was, it has presented us with a rich opportunity to teach the beauty of the human body and the grace necessary to respect and dignify the gift of our bodies. The abuse scandal has been an opportunity of significant grace. But church leadership has rejected this opportunity. We missed the chance.

Church ministry is organic. Reflecting this, the Office of the Separated, Divorced and Widowed later came under the umbrella of the Office of Social Concerns, the division of the diocese working with and educating about the seven principles of Catholic social teaching. The dignity of the human person, the call to community, the rights and responsibly of the human person, the dignity of work and the rights of workers, options for the poor and vulnerable, solidarity and care for God's creation: all are solidly based in scripture.

It was an easy transition for me, because justice and charity are main components of our faith. Most Catholics recognize the call to social action. The church's social justice ministry is a reflection of God's presence in the world.

The repositioning of my office took me to our state capital as well as to Washington, DC, to serve on committee after committee, trying to give voice to those treated unjustly. I wrote letters to the editor, to members of congress, and to those responsible for mediating the respect of all peoples. Sometimes my efforts worked. At other times, they fell flat or short, but never from a lack of trying.

My responsibilities now included developing and teaching about charity and justice and continuing to teach about alcoholism, recovery, and annulment. It was easy for me. Pounding nails; cooking food; hugging the elderly, the homeless, the veteran suffering from chemical dependency or mental illness. I now constantly faced people who simply wanted someone to love them. I met these people in homeless shelters and at food shelves. I worked to develop programs such as Habitat for Humanity and Christmas in April. I held a child with alcohol fetal syndrome and continued to provide care and treatment for their alcoholic parent, the families of alcoholics, the parishes and communities with suffering alcoholics. And more....

"We are God carriers," said Desmond Tutu. To believe that all human beings are God carriers is to believe that life is present from the womb to tomb. The work of social justice included addressing the elimination of all violence. Executions called for by the death penalty, therefore, eliminate a God carrier, as do abortions. How do we say abortion is wrong and the death penalty is permissible, even necessary? This is a contradiction. One recipient of the death penalty, during his execution, said, "Father, forgive them, for they know not what they do." His name was Jesus.

"My son is gay," the weeping mother told me as we walked from the church. I had just given a presentation about reconciliation at a retreat. In it, I talked about how our faith begs us to see with different eyes. I gave the example of the rejection of gay people. The mother continued, "If my community knew, we would be totally rejected." We talked and hugged. I assured her of my support. And I assured her that I would do what I could to continue educating within the church.

When I grew up, "gay" meant happy. Or it was a given name. I had no clue, until I was an adult, that the word had another meaning. At that time, no one I knew—and I mean no one—used the word in reference to sex. Today, we understand sexual orientation as something that is shaped in utero. A choice to be gay? I have never met one gay person who feels that he or she made the choice to be who he or she is. Quite the contrary. I see the paralyzing fear, the pain often causing the liver to be eaten away by alcohol or other drugs, the spirit destroyed.

Yet socially, the issue is anything but settled. The debate will continue ad infinitum. In the context of the church, homosexuality is a topic of great pain. Those condemning homosexual behavior quote the scriptures. People justify their prejudice. Politician use the subject, as they do abortion, to get elected. Few of these people truly understand the pain they cause when they damn and condemn fellow human beings just because they are gay.

It is often not until you either know someone or love

someone who has "come out" that you begin to understand the pain that homosexual people experience in the face of hatred and rejection. Sometimes they numb the pain with alcohol or other drugs. Or suicide. In my experience, the prejudice against homosexual orientation comes from ignorance, self-hatred, or often a person's fear of his or her own sexuality. And in my opinion, the church's treatment of the topic in light of the reality is disingenuous.

Catholics are sometimes uncomfortable believing that all of this is the work of the church. But it is the church. A church, a parish, is really a recovery community, a place that builds, shelters, and offers resources of kindness, forgiveness, and love. Lacking those elements, it is not a community of faith that truly reflects the "t" in "Catholic." Baptized Catholics are called to do works of charity and to speak to justice.

My faith and my church teaches all to be pro-human and to believe in the ethic that I heard Cardinal Joseph Bernadine describe more than once: woman, man, straight, gay, saint, sinner—every person is a God carrier. This is the simple message of the gospel that preaches that reaching out and loving make the difference.

Tim Russert, the compassionate, iconic newsperson, once said that the best exercise for the human heart is to reach down and pick another up. Father Flannigan knew this when he founded Boys Town. Father Cassidy knew it when he began Home on the Range for Boys. I knew it when I crossed a finish line in Chicago, having ridden 492 miles, along with 1,699 other cyclists, in the annual AIDS ride. The message comes from multiple sources.

The twelve steps of AA, the church's seven sacraments, the seven principles of Catholic social teaching: all preach that same message.

My finger pushed the doorbell. The door swung open.

"Go to the living room."

Obediently, I walked toward the spacious room. A small black bike stood in the center. Puzzled, I looked but said nothing. Father Anthony, a man of few words, handed me an envelope, his hand resting on the bike.

"Take this envelope. Go to a secondhand store." He told me which one he had in mind. He continued, "There is another, similar bike on hold there in your name."

I hesitated, then said, "Father, thank you. I cannot accept such a generous gift."

His brown eyes ablaze, he said, "This gift is for the children." He continued with uncharacteristically strong emotion, saying, "After the death of my father, daily I walked past a hardware store, looking wantonly at a shiny, red sled." He continued in a deep, muted voice. "On the farm, Mom worked alongside Dad until the day he died. She had to find a job. She found one cooking at the Catholic school. She tried to make ends meet. I knew we could not afford the sled." His voice quivered and looking away, he continued, "The store's owner, looking gruff and angry, waved me in. Trembling, I went."

Father continued, relating what the brusque German storeowner of his childhood said to him. "'Every day you stand outside my window and look at that sled. What's wrong with you?' he asked me in his stern voice. I was petrified. Words stuck in my throat. The owner moved toward me, reaching around me. He took the sled from the window and said, 'Merry Christmas,' handing me the treasured gift. I never forgot that moment."

He said gently, "The kids deserve a bike." I choked. No one was this good to us. I could not speak. And I certainly did not want Father to see me cry. He wasn't finished. "Take this envelope; use what is in it to pay for the bike." Uncomfortable, I was still unable to talk.

When I got to the shop, I opened the envelope to pay for the bike. Five one hundred dollar bills fell out. The bike cost forty dollars. Taken aback, I returned home with the bikes, along with the cash that remained after sales tax: $455. I called Father to express my gratitude and to decline the money.

"It was from my mother's estate. She would have been pleased to know she provided bikes to five kids. It is from Mom, and she won't take it back."

This man, this priest, over the next twenty-two years, introduced me to Cyrano De Bergerac, Thomas Merton, *The Seventh Story Mountain*. He had an address book filled with the names of family members, parishioners past and present, fellow priests and religious, all of whom he contacted or assisted in a myriad of ways. As his daily calendar showed, he was constantly busy, serving others, spiritually guiding others masterfully and with certitude.

Reading his breviary three times daily, this man of extraordinary prayer celebrated three masses on Saturday and three on Sunday, as well as a daily mass the other five days. He attended to the sick in the hospital and in nursing homes, parish council, the liturgy and finance committees, the school board, and the building committee. He advised those preparing for marriage. He officiated at funerals. He worked gently with his parish secretary and bookkeeper, as well as the support groups that met at the church.

He provided a pastor's ear at confessions; presided over Holy Week, the seasons of advent and lent; led the stations of the cross and vespers; and celebrated weddings and baptisms. He supplied down payments, tuition, food, shelter, and support to parishioners and people he never knew.

He had deep brown eyes that spoke to the truth of the saying "the eyes are the windows to the soul." They revealed a man of profound intelligence, of deep gentleness and care that derived from a deep longing. I learned this at our first meeting. I questioned why it was so dark in the rectory. I learned that he was sensitive to light and struggled with depression, which was probably rooted in the death of his beloved father in his childhood.

He loved children. He was the type of man that, had he married and become a father himself, only gentle Joseph could surpass. He also loved the Peanuts comic strip and its characters: Charlie, Linus, Lucy, and the rest. He said that he related to Charles Schultz and appreciated the psychological, emotional, and theological struggles of the Peanuts gang.

He loved baseball, the *New Yorker*, intellectual conversation, smoking the pipe, LL Bean, public radio, voting Democrat. And above all else, he loved his parish. His loyalty to and passion about his parish family came out in the passion he showed when anyone dare put it down. He often said of his parish, "It is the poorest, smallest, but best parish in the city." He was correct.

He was passionate about many things. He loved biking and was on his beloved bike almost daily. His canoe trips were favorites among family and friends. He loved birds, bird watching, and the significance of words attributed to Saint Francis of Assisi:

My sister birds, you owe much to God, and you must always and in everyplace give praise to God, for God has given you freedom to wing through the sky. God clothed you . . . you neither sow nor reap. God feeds you and gives you rivers and fountains for your thirst, and mountains and valleys for shelter, and tall trees for your nests. And although you neither know how to spin or weave, God dresses you and your children, for the Creator loves you greatly and blesses you abundantly.

A ferocious reader, he was a walking encyclopedia and had an extensive library housing of the work of C. S. Lewis, the classics, many biographies, *A Sand County Almanac*, Eric Sloane's books on wood. He loved Thomas Jefferson, another ferocious reader, and made him come alive when he spoke about him. In fact, I called him Tom, because of the similarities they shared.

He was also a rabid environmentalist. He had a piece of farmland outside the city that he called "the farm." There, he planted a garden, often using planting, sewing, weeding, harvesting, and loving the earth, activities he did daily, as metaphors for living the gospels.

OUR FINAL JOURNEY
Gentle Anthony,
Sitting,
saliva falling,
Color appalling,
Strength diminished.
Life now finished.
Anthony a man.
Anthony a priest.
Anthony a gift.

Heart strong, mind gone.
Now I see.
Why is he.
Gone not forgotten.
Alive sleeping.
This man who gave life meaning.

Father Anthony suffered a heart attack. At the hospital, he begged me to take him home. It was awful. Even the memory makes me physically sick. The memories flood my mind. The smile, the brown eyes, and the gentle, gentle heart.

He left me his journal. In it contained many things, including this note.

Dear Father, We enjoyed your sermon Saturday 5:15
Mass. It lifted us. We were going for a drink at the VFW.
Then we went to Mass instead.

 PS. We were glad that we went to Mass instead of
a drink.

It was signed: Grateful Parish Members. Such was the result of the gospel he lived.

We had fallen in love. We had fallen in love and stayed in love, although we never moved toward that love. We both knew that he was a priest first and always. He died a priest first and always. No matter how much we loved one another. He was a priest to the end. A good man. A good son. Brother. Uncle. Friend. A good priest. Most of his seminary classmates left and married. He supported their decisions and courage. His courage was evident in his staying. He was the best man I have ever known.

In Anthony's journal was another note.

Everyone is responsible but no one is to blame. Life is
a prolonged farewell. It is a continuous saying goodbye
and completing of cycles of growth. I am ready.

His last request of me: "Will you sing at my funeral?"

My heart bled, but I tried to keep it together, for both of us. "Anthony, you know I will do anything you ask."

He continued, "Will you sing 'Wherever You Go,'" It was a song made famous by the Weston monks from Vermont and one he felt strongly about. He asked. I did what he asked.

Wherever you go I shall go.
Wherever you live so shall I live.
Your people will be my people
And your God will be my God, too.
Wherever you die I shall die.
And there shall I be buried beside you.
We will be together forever
And our love will be the gift of our lives.

While he still lived, I made another promise: "I will care for you until the day you die." I did.

A priest is a man with all the foibles, struggles, and conflicts of any man, of any human. A priest is expected to do and be more. Sometimes in subhuman ways. When they fall short of the expectation for some people there is no room for forgiveness.

God is kind and merciful. Are we?

Anthony often paraphrased Charles Dickens's *A Tale of Two Cities* as we witnessed the pending, foreboding reality we see today in the church. He said, "We have known the best of times. And now we are going in to the worst." His words were prophetic.

Chapter 15

Dec. 20, 1993
Have no fear of moving into the unknown. Simply step out fearlessly knowing that I am with you, therefore no harm can befall you; all is very, very well. Do this in complete faith and confidence.
  —John Paul II

The prophetic words of John Paul played out in my shower, of all places. The smell of Paul Mitchell shampoo filled my nostrils as I showered, reflecting on my plans for the upcoming Christmas. I was jolted back to reality when something crashed through the shower curtain. Everything changed.

The morning had begun so differently, so normally. It was the end of advent, with Christmas waiting in the wing. I woke up at 5 a.m. to deliver the morning paper route. (I paid Catholic school tuition for my children in large part by the paper route.) All went as it always did.

When I returned home, I saw the caramels sitting on the counter, wrapped in wax paper, waiting to be delivered in the next days. Every Christmas, I made homemade caramels as an appreciation gift for each newspaper customer. This Christmas was no different.

Noticing that some were missing, I realized that the boys must have eaten some prior to going to sleep the night before; I wrapped more to complete the gifts.

I was running late; we all were. I woke up my two high-school-age children. They showered, had breakfast, and jumped in the car. That morning it was my turn to drive the neighborhood car pool to Saint Mary's, our local Catholic high school. My youngest son, an eighth grader at Saint Mary's grade school, was still at home, sleeping, when I returned from the car pool. Deciding to complete my morning ritual before waking him, I finished my morning meditation, breakfast, and got in the shower.

The sweet smell of the shampoo filled the air when a dark energy blasted through the shower curtain. A hand grabbed me around the neck. Through the shampoo, I could see a black ski mask. My first thought was that this was some kind of sick, cruel joke. Then I smelled the stale smell of alcohol. I could make out facial hair and menacing eyes.

I felt something cold against my throat. He said, "Do what I say or I will kill you." My maternal instincts took over, knowing my son was asleep in his room. But utter fear engulfed me. I thought, "If he finds my son, or my son attempts to protect me, a thirteen-year-old is no match against an adult with a knife."

My survival response kicked in. I struggled. The room swirled. I felt lightheaded, weak. I needed oxygen. Blood was everywhere. At the time, I didn't know if the blood was his or mine.

"Please, can we go to the other room where it will be more comfortable?"

I heard the words coming from my mouth. The tone of my voice did not match the terror in my body. I found an inner strength. I went on, "We must hurry. My neighbor will be here any minute." I could not believe what I was saying. No neighbor was coming. It was pure survival.

I had purposefully not used a pronoun when referring to the neighbor. I wanted to place doubt in my attacker's mind. Miraculously, the rapist agreed. The time it took for us to move gave me a moment to collect my thoughts. I began to use my momentary resources.

Rape, I knew, was not about sex, but rather about power and control. For a moment, I felt a sense of freedom. He pushed me onto the bed. Coming down on top of me, he tried to remove his penis from the tight spandex underwear he was wearing under a sweat suit.

I worked professionally with sex offenders. I could tell that this was not his first time. I also worked with the AIDS virus and was aware that he could infect me, possibly with deadly consequences. Again, I drew from an inner source. I was able to talk him into oral sex. If he agreed, I thought, I might reduce any chance of getting infected.

He stood and freed his penis, yelling at me to start. Then another miracle. I began to make soothing statements, appealing to his ego. "This is so wonderful. You are so good." The voice, the words, were mine, but they were coming from a place I did not know, a place of paralyzing fear. Nevertheless, I realized I was now controlling him.

Three distinct thoughts raced through my mind. The first was of my five children finding me in a pool of blood. They'd never recover if they found their mother dead. The second was of the Holocaust. I now knew, in a small way, what the women felt as they were tortured and raped. The third was of the pope.

In the middle of a rape, I thought about Pope John Paul II. "I want to forgive this man, like John Paul did his would-be assassin" was the prayer that emerged from deep within my soul. A peace came over me at that moment. I knew I would live.

"If I do this, will you leave?" I asked. Again, my voice sounded foreign, but I knew it was mine. With the knife flailing, he yelled, "Just do it." My plan was to run at the moment he ejaculated. Fortunately, I changed my plans.

Later, I discovered the rapist was a buff, muscular man. Even attempting an escape in the moment of weakness could have brought death. I gagged as I felt the warm fluid fill my mouth. "Don't throw up. Don't throw up," I kept telling myself. "He will kill you." I didn't. I let it fall from my mouth to the floor. His DNA, I thought.

His body went limp. He landed on top of me. Within seconds, his adrenaline restored, he grabbed me and threw me through the doorway to the bathroom. The knowledge of the room saved me. I jumped from his arms and slammed and locked the bathroom door. I yelled through the door that the neighbor was going to be there at any moment. Hearing nothing, I opened the door and saw the kitchen door ajar. I fled to the phone and dialed 911.

The voice on the end of the phone was the voice of God, gentle, soothing, and clear. "Breathe," it said. "An officer will be with you in a minute. Keep breathing."

I looked out the window, trying to do as the voice reminded me. The December death grip was playing out in the massive oak tree outside my window; it was stripped of its leaves, waiting spring. As I looked at that very dead, lifeless tree, I saw beauty. "I am alive," I kept repeating to myself.

Officer Michael Arnold arrived within minutes. Officer Jeff Azure apprehended the rapist a few minutes later. He had fled a block away, to a house where he was staying, to shower.

"My son is downstairs," I said to the officer. My voice sounded shrill, yet plaintive. My legs were shaking. Blood was everywhere. I was bleeding. I did not feel anything. I wanted to vomit.

Together we entered my son's room. Somehow, I managed an inarticulate noise that sounded like "Bret."

He tore from his bed. "Mom, what's wrong?"

The officer replied for me. "Son, your mother was attacked."

Bret flew into a rage. We held him until he released the anger. My mind raced, wanting to protect him. Police, detectives, and investigators arrived. Detectives Al Nass, Julie Thompson, and Dennis Walth. The name tags. Their badges. My small, neat little house filled with concerned, angry, yet professional officers. They asked questions.

I showed them. "There is his semen," I said. I walked the officers through the experience, pointing to evidence on the floor of the bedroom. They collected the evidence. Sealed it. I identified the shoes, the clothing. They never found the knife and ski mask. I felt dirty. Violated. My house, my sanctuary, had been polluted.

Officer Nass said, "Annetta, you are bleeding." It was then I noticed that all the blood was coming from me. The knife had been a filet knife. Every place he touched me, he sliced me. I hadn't felt it.

"We will call an ambulance."

"No," I said. "It will scare my elderly neighbor. I can drive myself to the emergency room, but I have to be at work." My mind and my body were in different places.

The prosecutor in the case, seasoned and brilliant, pursued justice. My children and the community provided support. I developed posttraumatic stress disorder (PTSD). For a long time, I continued to walk through the trauma. My spiritual advisor encouraged me to write about it. Friends called, brought food and warmth. Speaking publicly helped me to heal.

The terror of that morning came full circle when, originally pleading not guilty, the rapist changed his plea the night before jury selection was to begin. My children and I arrived at the courthouse to hear his plea, to face this person, and provided a letter. The prosecutor gave the letter to the judge, stating that if the rapist took the letter to heart, it might change him. It did not. The judge read the letter and handed it to the rapist. He open and read the words.

This is what the letter said.

Ron,

If on Dec. 20 you had knocked on my door, I would have given you food, shelter, clothes, even money. I have done that many times for many people. Instead, you chose actions that have altered both of our lives.

Ron, you know as well as I what you face upon your return to the pen. I pray there will be no more violence in you or done to you. I also pray when you receive help, you are honest and discover what has brought you to such insidious, sick behavior. You can manipulate the system as many do or you can choose to become a productive member of society. The choice is yours. I have sons. I never want to see any young person involved in this type of behavior. It destroys people's lives.

I do not hate you. I abhor your behavior. I pray for
you and ask you to pray for me.
  Annetta

When pleading guilty, he stated, "I went to her house for money. When I didn't find any, I decided to rape her." He continued, "I forced her into her bedroom at knifepoint and threatened to kill her if she didn't meet my demands."

The prosecutor stated to the local paper, "She (the victim) has, throughout this situation, been vital in the successful prosecution of this case. I am astounded and amazed at how well she has maintained herself during the process and dealing with the pressures of the assault. I am amazed at her courage. Very few people can take a tragedy and turn it into an attribute. And I don't say that about very many people."

The judge sentenced my attacker to twenty years. Later, he attempted escape. Shortly after the rape, I completed renovating my home. I then learned that he had placed a contract on my life and the lives of two states attorneys and two judges. I also learned that the others had security protection. I did not. The authorities also told me he knew where I lived. I sold my home.

PTSD arrives in waves. I made a decision to turn the terror to care. I worked with legislation for AIDS testing, reaching out to victims of assault and those suffering from trauma through my work in domestic violence shelters, treatment centers, and parishes. The rapist continues to serve time for ongoing crime sprees. Periodically, I come across the news reports of his crime sprees. He's released, and he reoffends and is again institutionalized.

Chemicals, marijuana, and alcohol filled the body of this man as he entered my home. Will he change? I am not the judge. Do I pray for him? Every day. Recently I received a call from a state attorney who was again prosecuting his crimes. The attorney reported to me, "Ron is serving a life sentence in increments."

"I want you to have this," the parish priest said, handing me a picture. Presenting an already scheduled retreat on reconciliation shortly after the rape, I told the story of my attack and the quieting influence of Pope John Paul. With tears in his eyes, the parish priest presented me with a picture of John Paul II and his would-be assassin during their prison meeting.

The eyes of both men tell the story. The eyes of Mehmet Ali Agca, the gunman. Those of John Paul. John Paul's hand shaking the hand that tried to kill him. Forgiveness. The gospel's call.

Evil persists in the world. I looked evil in the face that morning of my attack. The support of my children and the community brought me through the days that followed. My life was saved through faith. And Pope John Paul II.

"Do not abandon yourselves to despair. We are the Easter people and hallelujah is our song."
—Pope John Paul II

Chapter 16

Logan Airport, Boston. Our final destination. I looked across the seats; there they sat, teasing one another, laughing. Amazing. Five of them. The plane landed.

I had come to love Boston's Logan Airport. To love Boston, so often the scene of dreams just getting under way: college for Jenny, a master's program for her mother. History. And everything Kennedy, the imperfect family who is reflected in the pictures on my walls and in the books in my home.

This trip was special. I had completed my master's program at Emmanuel College. The six of us were coming together to celebrate the milestone. This leg of the journey was over. We had walked an implausible journey. Joy, affection, fear, abuse, abandonment. The six of us were together to celebrate.

"Parents are God's babysitter," Bishop Fulton J. Sheen said passionately on his long silenced weekly TV program. With no personal knowledge, the words of a master revealed a truth. Children never belong to us. Parents plant seeds and provide the direction, stability, security, nurturance, love, and affection. Children are the sponges. Mine soaked it all up. I willingly provided all I could.

Grieving in parenthood begins at conception. Children will eventually leave. A woman who gives birth, or any mother, knows it, although for awhile she may be in denial. Letting go is a daily event. Children are never really ours. It is an illusion to think otherwise.

My heart burst as I saw them on the plane. It was the same sensation I had experienced the days of their births. An experience of the Divine. A glimpse of God.

I was reminded of another trip. The five were small when we visited Pikes Market in Seattle. The event was my brother's wedding. A calligrapher was penning a document for a customer. I stepped at his side to watch. He looked up and said, "Give me five words."

"God, heart, children, mother, joy," I said.

From those five words, he wrote,

Amy, Emy, Jenny, Chet and Bret. You are the petals of my flowering—each beautiful, each unique, and each loved. You are God's gift to me—the gift of love. God gave to humankind a partnership in creation each new life created is created so that another may share in the Joy of knowing an everlasting Love. As each of you grows, I daily pray that you share in God's Love. And when the time comes that you are on your own I daily pray that you remember that God is always there, waiting with His Love to share.

"On their own" had come too quickly. Our Boston trip, I knew, was the last time it would be just the six of us. There would be marriages, families of their own. More immediately there were pending graduations, college entrance, and future plans for their adult lives. This trip was special. I had a plan to celebrate the journey and the mother—child bond I shared with each.

We arrived at Faneuil Hall and visited Celtic Weavers, the Irish shop. I wanted us to celebrate with an Irish tradition. Claddagh rings. I presented one to each of my children. Saint Joseph and I had culminated our jobs.

⁓

"Mom, do we have to go to church?"

As my children became teenagers, I heard this response often as we prepared for Mass on Sunday mornings.

"No, you don't HAVE to. You are so fortunate that you get to," I'd reply cheerfully.

"Mom, will you give me my diploma?"

"Mom, will you come to the University of Saint Thomas for a parent's event?"

"Mom, will you come to Boston to attend a mother–daughter brunch at Simmons?"

And now there she was, my oldest, manager of a large department store. I look for her by scanning the top of the racks for her moving head, finding her by recognizing her ever-present energy.

And then another reality.

⁓

"Mom, I am in detox."

As my oldest son slipped into the disease of alcoholism, I thought I knew what to do. My efforts to help began when he shared with me the story of the first night he took a drink of alcohol. He was almost apologetic. How many times had we discussed alcoholism? It's impact on our family? The genetic predisposition? A knot formed in the pit of my stomach. We talked. He kept saying, "I know, Mom. I know."

A few weeks before, he made his first visit to the Twin Cities to attend a Twins baseball game. He was the proud owner of his first car. I was supportive, but nervous. I placed a note in the snacks I packed. It offered a mother's love and instruction:

Call home collect if any problems. Call Emy if you get lost—she knows every inch of Minneapolis. Fasten seat belt in Minnesota—it's the law. Call when you get there. Drive 55–60 mph. Keep your doors lock and don't give any hitch-hikers a ride. When you stop for gas, do so at a station with many people.

Today I hold those innocent moments of motherhood with my oldest son deep in my heart.

The sun was bright as they sat a chair in the middle of the driveway. "Mom, sit here."

The last graduation. Bret's. I sat down and they presented me with a plaque. It read,

Thank you for sticking with it for twenty-seven years. These photographs reflect what a wonderful job you have done so far with the earned title . . . Mom.
Thanks, Mom
Your 'Troops'

It was written beautifully in my new son-in-law's handwriting.

My response was a letter.

Amy, Emy, Jenny, Chet, and Bret,

    This thank-you letter has been long in coming; nonetheless, it is filled with gratitude. Thank you, my children, for the wonderful plaque and gift of dishes. I will treasure it always. I show everyone and cry every time I read it. There is no mother on the face of this earth that has more pride or love for her children.

    Our lives are changing so rapidly. I know change is a part of life. Many times, it is good; sometimes it is painful. Letting all of you go has been the most difficult. My main goal as a mother has always been to help you seek a secure sense of self and independence. I never wanted to control your lives or suffocate you. I know that feeling, never wanted my children to feel it. Consequently, there may at times be the feeling that I am apathetic toward a given child or situation. The opposite is true, I experience tremendous pain, but I try to keep my mouth closed and pray.

    For twenty-seven years, you have been my life. The thought of you growing up has always been difficult. Every minute of your lives from the time you were conceived, I cherished you. I would marvel in every tiny thing you did, from a coo, to your teeth, to you first words, to your conversations with each other, to your first days of school, to your ballgames, your swimming, gymnastics, homework, friends who changed your lives drastically. There is a passage in scripture that talks about Mary holding these things in her heart. All of those memories

I've held in my heart. They are a big part of whom I am.
You, each of you, I hold deep within my heart.

Yes, there have and will continue to be many
changes in our lives. People entering, people leaving.
One thing will remain constant and that is the fact that
we are family. You will always find strength in family.
There will and have been times we have hurt each other
and we need to say I am sorry. We also need to accept
that. Life is too short to remain angry at trivial hurts.
Life is too precious and sacred not to live it to the fullest.
Every moment of every day.

Every one of you so unique. You all have your own
beauty and individuality, yet you all have so much in
common. The words of God are important: "Love one
another as I have loved you." Said by God but also by
your mother.

ILY
Mom

When I wrote the letter, the house was empty. Quite.

Chapter 17

Confirmation of reality and reconciliation often occur in stages.

A few years before Dad died, he and I were visiting when, unexpectedly, he said, "I have never understood why your mother has been so hard on you."

We had been talking about the severe punishment I had received from him as a child. He told me that he felt bad about it, regretted it. I knew immediately what he was referring to.

I was entering my junior year of high school. Mother had given permission for my sister Vonnie and me to have sodas with two boys. When Dad returned from serving a sheriff's warrant, she told him that she did not know where we were. It was a lie. She had given us permission and she knew it, but was attempting to save face with Dad. It was something Mom would do to protect herself from something she had done that Dad might have not have appreciated. This time, I received the beating.

When he told me he regretted it was one of those sacred moments of healing. I always gave my father a pass on any punishment he doled out, because I knew my mother instigated it and I knew the strength of my mother's persuasion. Although he was responsible for his own actions, Mom was like a rat terrier, biting at his heels. He would take it for a long time and then he'd break. When he broke, I, more than once, was the casualty.

My oldest brother, Wally, during an unusual point in our adult relationship, called me after attending a court-ordered alcohol-counseling class, "You are the scapegoat in our family," he had said.

I laughed out loud. It was not a shock to me. Some of my younger siblings shared mother's feelings toward me. My youngest brother, Joe, told me as he was dying, "Mom was hard on you." Those five words, shared during a consecrated, holy time together, confirmed my feeling emotionally disinherited. I just smiled. Family healing occurs at interesting intervals. It did in mine.

My mother's feelings toward me. It took years of recovery before I understood that I was a reminder of the man who had died and left her with four babies.

It had always been difficult for her to talk about Dad's death. Early in life, Mom told me I looked like my biological father, that I was a carbon copy of his mother, my grandmother Emelie. As a child, I was told that I looked and acted like Dad's older sister, Amelia, whom I adored. Mother had loved Dad. Other than her brothers and two sons, she compared every man who ever came through her life to him.

My sister Karren's husband, Dennis, came the closest. She also compared my second father to my first. This angered me. I loved my first dad. I missed him my entire life. But since I knew my second father longer, I adored him. I know Mom loved both husbands, even though they were two very different men.

Unprocessed grief affected our entire family and ravaged relationships throughout our family. Grief also played a part in the strength of religious faith in the family. Wally completely lost his faith. Mine has sustained me. Mom relied on it, often contradicting, at least in my eyes, what she said with what she did. Dad shared it, with his grace and compassion. The rest of the family fell somewhere in between.

In one way or another, all of our hearts were scarred. Sometimes I thought that the anger my mother felt toward me had started in her head and then exploded in her heart, due to the tremendous loss of her first love. Later, my marriage to Jack sealed the deal and my relationship with Mom. Mom's utter disdain for my husband was rooted in his treatment of our children and his treatment of me in the throes of alcoholism. For many reasons, Mom told me not to marry Jack. I did not listen.

It was the first overt rebellion of my life. Later, she told people that the only thing that would keep her from heaven is her hatred for my husband. Years later, this imperfect, remarkable woman even took care of that. Life was changing in a myriad of transitions. Several were waiting.

"I am going to see Dad," I stated to Bev, my executive assistant and friend.

"Is he worse?" she asked. She knew about the numerous medical scares during his advanced emphysema.

"No. I just want to see him." Planning to attend a meeting in Fargo, I first made a horseshoe trip to Watertown to visit Dad. It proved to be a sacred visit. Our last.

Before I left him for my meeting in Fargo, I pressed my lips on his cheek, choking back tears deep in my soul. His eyes filled with tears. He said, "I love you, baby." It was a phrase he didn't often say.

My heart was breaking. The thought of this man who had provided me with more than I could even describe leaving this world was too much. "I love you too, Dad," I managed to say.

I cried all the way to Fargo.

Seven days later, my sister called and said, "You'd better come." Wally and I began the three-hundred-mile trip on a beautiful, warm October evening. An hour out of Watertown, I felt an overwhelming warmth go through my body as I looked at the moon and prayed. As we drove down the familiar Arrow Avenue in Watertown, a hearse was driving the other way. I choked. A deep pain in the depths of my soul combusted. A wail. "No. No."

We wanted to have a wake and rosary in Watertown, then take Dad home to his beloved Corson County for his funeral and burial. The funeral directors planned a transfer of his body midway between the two places. I startled my entire family when I announced, "We will not allow an impersonal transfer of Dad's body from one hearse to another. We will find a suburban, remove the seats, and place Dad in the back. We will take Dad home."

The shocked expressions on the faces told me their feelings. I decided that if anyone found it too difficult to ride with me, Dad and I could do it together. Mother and Dad taught me how to handle death and the process that followed. I knew I could do it. Joe, my brother, offered to ride with me. The procession, twelve vehicles long, traversed the three hundred miles it took to take Dad home. He and I led the way.

I drove first pass the jail and the courthouse, then our old hotel, and then up the main street that Dad had walked, talked, and driven on all those years. We arrived at the church in which he had knelt and prayed, received the Eucharist, cried for his daughters, and modeled to everyone the things that matter in the home and family, in his county and church. He had been a minister with a badge.

The first tribute to him that I wrote was the essay in high school that got him recognized as King of the Dads. My second I gave at his funeral. As I moved toward the lectern in Saint Bonaventure, my heart exploded in grief.

"It is good to be home," I heard myself say. "Saint Bonaventure is the place Mom and Dad helped build. It is where we celebrated baptisms, Communions, confirmations, weddings, and, yes, funerals. We never believed today would come. Our dad was bigger than life. He was never going to leave us.

"How do you eulogize a man who represented God to us? A man who showed us the hands and face of God in everything he did. A man who never went to college yet had more intelligence than any PhD I know. He was a psychologist, psychiatrist, theologian, doctor of education, contractor, mechanic, architect, counselor, doctor of medicine (he was the only sheriff in the world who carried an oxygen tank in the trunk of his car for anyone who needed a little shot of air), and even a photographer.

"In an age in which we too often hear of parents abandoning, abusing children, this man accepted the responsibility of four fatherless children and gave life to three more.

Dozens more he fed, clothed, and sheltered. Mom says, 'A thirty-six-year-old bachelor, he married into chaos and has known chaos ever since.'"

I continued. My throat swelling. Eyes brimming. Unable to look at Mom, Wally, Joe, Mary, Cece, or my children. "His belongings could be placed in a cardboard box, because he never bought anything for himself. He was too busy taking care of us and everyone else. We could always look out and see his face alongside Mom's at our piano recitals, ballgames, and concerts. Our education was important to Dad. He hauled more trunks and boxes into dorms and encouraged us when things were rough.

"He spent thousands of dollars for music lessons, driving eighty miles round trip on a Saturday so we could receive piano lessons from the Benedictine nuns in Lemmon, South Dakota. He would drive six hundred miles in one day to dance with his daughters at father–daughter dances at Saint Martin's.

"Our family trips were legend. Dad always said that even if he had to borrow the money, we would go on a family vacation every year. He called these trips 'getting out of jail,' since that it was the only time we left the jail, since someone—preferably the sheriff—had to be there at all times. He was not one for mushy stuff, yet on Easter morning, we woke up to Dad sitting at a table covered with Easter corsages for Mom, his daughters, and granddaughters.

"Next to Mom, his children, grandchildren, and great-grandchildren, he loved the people of Corson County the most. He loved every inch of its soil. Not trained in law enforcement, he received on-the-job training. He always said he was a peace officer, not a police officer. He never carried a gun and did not like locking people up, so consequently, sometimes they left. In layperson's terms, they had 'escaped,' only to send a postcard back to let us folks know where they were so we would not worry.

"Dad often took prisoners sentenced by the court to the South Dakota State Penitentiary in Sioux Falls. Each of us kids took turns being the 'guard.' Once it was our little brother, Joe's, turn to be the guard; he was nine or ten years old. Joe later shared, 'I was falling asleep in the back seat, and Dad and the prisoner were visiting. When I woke up, the prisoner was driving and Dad was resting his eyes!' How many inmates drive themselves to prison?

"We celebrate a man whose ever-present faith buoyed his life. On Sunday morning, no matter how late he came home from patrolling, we were at Mass Sunday morning. Harry Kittelson was a minister with a badge. He was a man of forgiveness. He taught that nothing was so bad that you couldn't sit down over a cup of coffee, visit, and reconcile the issue.

"He loved the Indian people of Standing Rock. He spent hours in Bullhead, Little Eagle, and Wakapala. The only request he had for his funeral was to have an Indian tradition, to have the dirt placed one shovel at a time. His children and grandchildren will honor his request.

"In closing, we thank you for celebrating with us the man we love. Two other expressions of gratitude are extremely important. The first to our mother, who walked with Dad as his partner for forty-five years and stood by his bed in death. Together, you taught us how to love. The other is our baby sister, Cece, brother-in-law Jim, our nephews and niece, Joshua, Mariah, and Isaiah. We can never thank you enough for being the ones who constantly cared for Dad. You responded to a sacred trust that our parents would be cared for at home. We can never repay you.

"Harry Kittelson was a man of common sense, integrity, who never forgot the roots from where he came. He was a gift from God."

Dad's keys to life were simple: be honest, use common sense, be faithful, eat as a family at the table for lunch and dinner, pray before you eat, make sure everyone has a place at the table, and stay at the table until the meal is finished. No grazing. Eat what is prepared and do not waste. Do your chores. Be respectful, especially to your mother. And go to church.

When Joe my brother and others have said, "You are the most like Dad," I have taken it as the greatest compliment I could ever receive. I can only pray to be the model he was for me. Ernie Larsen, the prolific writer on life and recovery wrote, "You practice what you learn. What you learn, you practice. What you practice, you become. And what you become has consequences." I pray that the consequences of the influence of Harry Kittelson on me show in my life, as I work to imitate a man who showed human decency and integrity.

Edwin Milton Royle 1862–1942, American playwright wrote words Dad often sang to us. A philosophy he lived. And a flower he loved. Later it became our official family song.

SUNFLOWER AIN'T A DAISY A MELON AIN'T A ROSE
A sunflower ain't a daisy. A melon ain't a rose.
Why is they all so crazy to be something else that grows?
Just stick to the place you were planted
and do the best you knows.
Be a sunflower or a daisy a melon or a rose.

After Dad's death sunflowers keep showing up.

Two short years later, I said another good-bye.

I was preparing dinner. The rich smell of roasting beef, garlic, celery, and onion wafted through the air. The vegetables were nestled, roasting, beside the grass-fed beef. The warmth of home. The potatoes were peeled, the salad made. Fresh bread rested on the counter, and the table was set. My spotless home was simply waiting the arrival of my mother and brother.

The phone rang. Sobs kept me from distinguishing any words. Then I recognized the voice. It was Joe.

"Mom is dead. Annetta, she is gone."

I could not speak. After what seemed like an eternity, everything went dark.

My mother. Dead.

It happened twelve hours before she was coming to spend a week with me. Joe, my youngest brother, had driven from the Twin Cities to Watertown, South Dakota, Mom and Dad's home for the last fifteen years. Joe, with the help of Cece, placed Mom in the car for the three-hundred-mile drive first to Lemmon, so they could decorate the graves, and then to my home. It became a life-changing trip for Mom, Joe, and the rest of her clan. The world changed in a few hours.

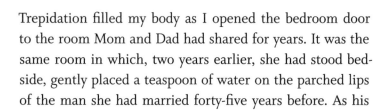

Trepidation filled my body as I opened the bedroom door to the room Mom and Dad had shared for years. It was the same room in which, two years earlier, she had stood bedside, gently placed a teaspoon of water on the parched lips of the man she had married forty-five years before. As his life slipped away from hers, she provided constant care and comfort. It was her final testimony in a history of her standing with him and his standing with her. They were faithful to one another to the end.

For two years, she had slept alone in the big bed.

I took a deep breath. My breath—the breath she had given me so long ago—was hauntingly short. Mom's smell lingered. My breath became even shorter gasps. It became difficult to breath.

In the dimly lit room, I saw it. It was nestled between votive candles and a myriad of frames. One picture. Of me. No frame, just the photo. My eyes filled with tears as I turned to my younger sister and asked, "I have never seen that picture. Where did it come from?"

A perplexed look passed across Cece's face. Cece. The youngest born, the one who provided constant, gentle, daily care for Mom. Cece, my baby sister. "I don't know," she said. "I didn't notice it this morning when I was helping Mom get ready."

Mom's last act. A picture. Placed there by her hands, the hands I would recognize anywhere, with the long nails she sometimes used as a weapon. This time her hands had moved gently, to carefully display a keepsake. It was a message to me. Tears streamed down my cheeks.

Her husbands, children, and grandchildren knew her as a woman of intense faith, liberal politics, and conservative values. Strong, controlling, loving, extroverted, and compassionate. She was a contradiction. A dichotomy. She loved to pray, gamble, debate, crochet, bake, cook, and feed anyone coming through the door.

Never understanding how addiction could be a disease, she had her own response to alcoholics: "Maybe they drank a little too much." And if the alcoholics were male, she'd make an exception, accept excuses. I am sure this stance was an unconscious way of protecting her five brothers who we all knew "drank too much."

Family was everything to Mother. She passionately loved family. She always wanted us to come home; in fact, she never wanted us to leave. As any of us departed from a visit home, Mom would stand on the doorstep, tears flowing, waving her arms until the car was out of sight.

This woman buried her parents, three children, five brothers, and two husbands. While she never let the tragedies of her life destroy her, those dark family dramas completely consumed every cell of her being. She was our family's Rose Kennedy, who, like the original, prematurely buried many of those she loved. And both were women who drew from their deep faith. And both were emotionally disconnected from their second children, Rose from her second son and LaVerna from her second daughter, me.

I learned of her harsh, difficult, early life from the pages of her journal. Only then did I fully appreciate that Mom came by her strength naturally. She passed that strength on to her fourth born.

"My God," I kept saying, page after page. I also found in her journal a list of people she prayed for daily. She had noted the name of every family member and friend. Tucked in among the names: Jack. She often said to anyone who'd listen that the one thing that would keep her from heaven was her hatred for Jack, my husband of ten years, the father of my five children. The man who abused her daughter.

She had avoided speaking to him for over twenty-five years. However, before her death, she gave Jack a letter.

Jack, I want to apologize for all the horrible things I have said about you over the years. I ask your forgiveness. I also forgive you for the horrible things you did to my daughter and my five grandbabies. I also want to thank you for giving me five of the most beautiful grandchildren anyone could have.

She signed it LaVerna. In the envelope she had slipped a rosary. It was a statement, a message, of forgiveness. Jack came to her funeral.

The last week of Mom's life, we had gathered in Denver for my niece's graduation. If any human has a premonition of death, Mom did. She was relaxed throughout the entire turbulent plane ride. Mom did not like flying, yet during this flight, she was completely at ease.

We shared a room in Denver. Sunday morning, prior to leaving for Mass, I entered our room while Mom was quietly saying her daily prayers. She looked up and asked, "Will you make me a promise?" This was unlike her. "Will you promise me Mariah will be protected?" Mom already knew the answer.

She was referring to Cece and Jim's little girl, who was special to all of us. Mariah represented God. Mom shared with me the saint she prayed to for Mariah's protection: Saint Fastenina. While Mom's theology differed radically from mine, I deeply respected the way her faith provided her with strength, just as my own faith sustains my life.

When we arrived back in South Dakota from Denver, I placed Mom in Cece's van at the airport for the drive home. I said, "Mom, I love you."

"I love you, too, honey."

Ironically, Mom's last earthly trip was coming to spend a week with me. She died of congestive heart failure on the way to my home. The night she died, I slept in her bed, as I did the night Dad died, alongside the picture of the small child, her fourth born, her nemesis.

In placing the photo there, at her own beside, I felt as if Mom said to me, "I love you." We had come full circle, Mom and me.

~

"Joe, the suit looks beautiful."

Through his tears, he said, "I know. I know." The devoted son was filled with grief. He had bought the suit for Mom some time before, for my daughter Emy's wedding. Mom had told Cece she wanted to be buried in it.

Mom had been dressed reverently. Her beloved rosary wrapped her hands. Her hands. Her hands were her résumé. The perfectly manicured nails. She had held her children, cooked, made celebrations, responded in love to her husbands, and prayed with those hands. No longer. And those long nails no longer a weapon. She has used those hands one last time in a gesture of love.

At her funeral Mass, her five children gave the homily. Her children, my siblings, shared their perspectives and their love of and for our mother, their perspectives so different from my own. My grief was different. Refined. Almost pleasant. Her grandchildren and great-grandchildren carried her coffin. We buried her by Dad, her partner and husband of forty-five years, as well as by two of her daughters, a grandchild, her own parents, and two of the five "boys." Her grandparents, Anne and James Tracy, lay close by.

We had said a rosary for her and prayed the Mass. In her eulogy, I had spoken my words carefully, thoughtfully:

"For a number of years I have wanted to write a tribute. I struggled with encapsulating the life of a woman born on the North Dakota prairies, raised during the Depression on desolate farmland in South Dakota. Orphaned with her five brothers at fifteen, left destitute, yet working her way through beauty school.

"She married a man she loved, giving birth five times, one baby dying three days after birth. Then she was shockingly, tragically widowed as a young woman with four small children. She married again, this time to a man who dedicated his life to her, her four children, and the three more born to their union.

"She was one of the first business women in her town—if truth be told, perhaps in the state. She became the deputy sheriff when her husband became sheriff, and for thirty-two years worked by his side. She raised not only her own children but also hordes of others who needed a mother.

"Her youngest daughter said of her, 'She could make a feast out of a turkey bone and a little flour.' And she could make the most exquisite celebrations out of a barren tree and a few blown-out, colored eggs. She called it an Easter egg tree.

"She was the most ecumenical person I have ever met, yet Catholicism was her life. It coursed through her veins. Both husbands were raised Missouri Synod Lutherans and converted to Catholicism, not because she demanded it, but because they wanted what she had. The rosary beads played across her fingers like the crochet hook and knitting needles with which she made brightly colored woolen caps, mittens, Afghans, and doilies for her children and grandchildren.

"Her Irish wit was legendary" and her sense of fun came out in a multitude of ways. She also was tough. She was like an FBI agent who never went to the academy. She taught that what's right always wins, although it might take awhile. To her, the important thing was to do what was right, not what was popular.

"She had a passion for politics and religion, feeling strongly that one should live one's religion, and that it should be reflected in what one did in society. On the day of her death, she was on the way to decorate her husbands' and daughters' graves, and then to come to my home for dinner.

"She was my mom."

I began to feel in the depths of my soul a deep emotion, a resolution, a love I had never experienced before. I continued.

"Mom, here we are at the end of a long road together. So many things, so little time. Mom, you truly were the 'foster mother.' You fostered family and faith, and you fostered forgiveness. From the time I was small until the day you died, you always wanted us to come home and you never wanted us to leave.

"Our road together was sometimes bumpy. Karren used to say it was because we were so much alike. Perhaps so.

"I do know that my life's work has come from you: feeding the hungry, sheltering the homeless, visiting the sick, comforting the sorrowful, setting prisoners free. Yes, Mom, a master in ministry, taught me.

"You also taught me to love like the Irish and work like a German. More than anything, you, a woman who lost her mother so young, taught me how to be a mother and grandmother.

"I pray:

May the road rise up to meet you.
May the wind be always at your back.
Until we meet again.
May God hold you in the palm of his hand.
I love you, my mother."

Mom and Dad taught us how to live, imperfect though they were. They also taught us how to die with dignity and grace.

~~~~

The phone rang. A familiar voice said, "Hi, Annetta." It was Patrick Joseph. Hearing his voice brought up the same feeling I had had that day at Mass so long ago.

"Patrick, I need to know: what happened?" Forty years of questions, angst, and sadness pealed away as he shared with me what had moved him to end our relationship so abruptly: multiple unresolved issues and parental control.

Forty years later, he explained what had prompted that letter. His mother had suffered from mental illness, and not only I, but many members of her family, had been impacted by a woman who had not received help, who, in her marriage, was the partner who didn't benefit from finding recovery.

Speaking with Patrick, I recalled the lesson I had learned from that hateful letter. Words can make or break our spirit. I had allowed her cruel words to keep me in a corner, to silence my voice. She taught me how the written word can be a source of construction or destruction. I eventually chose construction. She, without knowing it or wanting it, was one of my teachers.

As for her son and I, we rekindled our teenage friendship. It felt good.

~~~~~~

Graduations ceded to weddings as my children found life partners. For my girls, the place reserved for a father to give his daughters away was empty. Without hesitation, Amy, Emy, and Jenny asked me to do the honors. It was bittersweet. I was painfully aware of their loss. My lack now was theirs; just as I had had no biological father to walk me down the aisle, neither did they. And while I never received a wedding necklace from a father, neither did they receive a strand of pearls from theirs. But my heart was also filled with joy for each. They had chosen wisely and married well. I gained three incredible son-in-laws.

"Mom, I met the woman I am going to marry," my youngest son told me in a phone call from a retreat he was attending.

"Honey, that's wonderful," I replied. "Is she aware of this?"

Without hesitation, he replied, "No, but she will be." Little over a year later, it was my son's turn to say, "I do."

When a son marries, the role of a mother is very specific. Fathers usually provide the advice, the talk. I thought of Saint Joseph. I decided to write Bret a letter and present it prior to the wedding. I began:

My Son,

The day has arrived. It is different this time than the first time I let you go. That was to your first-grade teacher. This is different for many reasons. You now will know the total love of God through the total love of

Nicole and the children I know God will give you. There is no other love that can compare, other than the love of God and the love that brought you to this world. Yes, Bret, I know you were not privy to witness that love, but it was there; it gave you and your sibling's life.

Pardon my awkwardness, since fathers are usually the ones that either write or say the words I am about to say. The fact that you were not privileged to have such a relationship has given you a strength that many men never know. The day you were born, it was like you knew. You knew instinctively a gentleness and sensitivity that your siblings and mother have loved. I never worried about you being cruel. Never had to. My only concern was that, with the gentleness you have, you might get hurt. Instead, you have used it to love and provide kindness to others.

You were named after gentle Saint Joseph. Continue to emulate him.

Son, you are marrying your best friend. I knew immediately why you fell in love with Nicole. I loved her, too, the minute I met her. We all know our family is blessed with her presence. I would be remiss as your mother though, my son, if I did not share with you the things which are important to make your beautiful wife happy. They are things she may never say, but as a woman and your mother, I know they are important.

Women need to talk. Let her. Just listen. Sometimes you can't fix what she is feeling; just let her talk. Hold her, no matter what—every day.

Tell her how beautiful she is, no matter what her hair, nails, clothes, and body look like. Every woman wants to know that the man in her heart feels and

*thinks she is the most beautiful woman in the world,
even when she knows she is not. I know it makes no
sense—just do it. Be passionate. Always be passionate.*

*Never, ever, ever say anything that can even be con-
sidered a put down. Honor your wife. Respect and love
her. She will return that respect and love.*

This one is easy. Always respect her family.

*Never stop dating her. Never stop being affection-
ate. Never stop telling her you love her. Make every day,
even the bad ones, good by telling her how much you
love her and how important she is to your life.*

*And always pray together. Realizing that that
everything you do is a prayer. Keep God as the center of your life. And remember what both a wise priest
and your grandmother taught: the family that prays
together stays together.*

ILY, Mom

<hr />

I had based the mission of my office at the diocese on Micah
6: "What does God ask of you...?" It was with a sense of
having completed a God-given task when, on June 1, 2003,
that I wrote in resignation letter, "It is with great regret that,
after nineteen years, I resign my diocesan position."

The bishop's response read, in part,

*I also appreciate your visit some weeks ago regarding
your thoughts preliminary to this final decision. When
you framed your remarks as "good news and bad news,"
I told you that the only good news was that it would help
the budget; the bad news remains: that you would be*

leaving after all these years of service to the church in our diocese. You have been clearly the most visible member of our staff in the community. I am sure many people are indebted to you for your relentless and solid presentation of the gospel of social justice.

I am proud to say that his words spoke the truth.

Chapter 18

Joe's snowmobile accident all those years ago on Santa Claus Day seemed like just a youthful mishap compared to what happened many moons later. It was a warm, sunny Minnesota Sunday morning. Father's Day. We had planned a family cookout.

After Mass, I stopped at home to pick up some food I had already prepared. The phone rang. It was Joe. He was crying.

"I am in the hospital."

The call began our final journey together. I flew to the hospital. My impeccably handsome brother was sobbing.

"Annetta, my liver is gone."

My daughters and I began to surround Joe. We took care of him. Mary and Cece came when they were able. Joe was diagnosed with liver failure followed was hepatic encephalopathy. As the ammonia level in his blood increased, his life force decreased. His stomach enlarged with fluid. My baby brother was slipping away. The doctors discussed a transplant.

He went to ICU and then was moved back to the floor, only to be placed in ICU again. I took him home and then came the last coma. It occurred at my home. I called 911. First responders, professional and compassionate, worked to bring my brother back. As they loaded him on the stretcher,

I called to them, "Please cover my little brother. He gets so cold," sobs bursting from my throat.

He maintained his humor throughout. He told me, "If I live through this, I know I will need treatment."

I responded, "Let's take this a day at a time."

A few days later, he died.

The bells of the basilica rang as his coffin was brought down the steps. It was one place where he had felt a sense of acceptance for being who he was.

I prepared another eulogy.

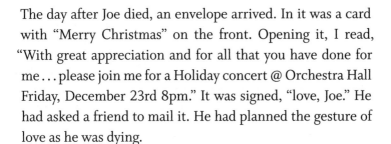

The day after Joe died, an envelope arrived. In it was a card with "Merry Christmas" on the front. Opening it, I read, "With great appreciation and for all that you have done for me . . . please join me for a Holiday concert @ Orchestra Hall Friday, December 23rd 8pm." It was signed, "love, Joe." He had asked a friend to mail it. He had planned the gesture of love as he was dying.

Shortly after Joe's funeral, I went on a mission trip to Haiti.

It was like balm for a grieving spirit. However, on the way home, sleep escaped me. The desperate cries of children, hungry, naked, and bloated, with empty eyes, floated through my head as I attempted to rest. I could still smell the human waste. Rum. I could still taste abject poverty. I could not sleep.

I kept seeing Emerson's face. The tiny baby I had fallen in love with, and he with me. Mother Teresa's sisters who ran the children's home had said, "Put him in your suitcase." They knew my heart. They also knew that, due to the political situation, the impossibility of me taking him with me or being able to adopt him. For the days we were together, Emerson knew a mother's total love. I baptized him Emerson Joseph.

As I closed my eyes, I felt the tired, emaciated bodies of the Haitian children in my arms. I saw the big black eyes looking at me, searching. My arms had held them tight. My heart now held them tighter. I wept.

Landing in Miami, I saw the immense amount of food, the signs reading, "Cover your cough." I noticed the state licenses for food safety. The children I left never experienced such security. No one was there to cover their coughs or keep their food safe.

On my connecting flight to Minnesota, the man seated next to me chatted about inane inconveniences of air travel. He inquired about my travel.

"Did you have fun in Florida? Enjoy the sun? Or do you live there?"

The questions flew. "I am returning from Haiti," I said. Silence. A few moments passed before he continued.

"Why would you go to Haiti?"

Knowing from the question that he probably wouldn't understand, no matter what I said, I responded, "We have a school in Leogone."

Undeterred, he continued, "School? What kind of school?"

I explained. He listened attentively. I also shared with him the outreach work I was doing at Mother Teresa's Children's Home. I told him how I initially had gone there to learn and support. It became much more.

He asked, "Are you with an organization?"

I responded, "A church. A parish."

"What church?"

"Catholic," I replied. There was a pregnant pause.

His said, "You know what bothers me about you Catholics?" I winced. I knew that the hour and half to travel back to Minneapolis was going to be too a long time to hear the horrors of what, why, and who. I braced myself, breathed deeply, said a prayer, and replied, "Tell me, what bothers you about us Catholics?"

"Well, I'm Baptist. But you Catholics do so much good and no one hears about it. Like this." He waived his hands feverously. "Why doesn't this land in the newspapers instead of all the dirt, the pedophile priests, what Rome does and doesn't do. This is something impacting lives and no one knows about it."

Surprised, I responded, "We don't do it to let people know. We do it because it is what we are called to do and be." There was another moment of silence.

"Oh," he said. I could tell that he got it. Some people don't.

Chapter 19

The call came as I was taking Joe home for burial. He had requested a funeral at the basilica, with cremation and burial back in Greenhill Cemetery in Lemmon to follow. I was taking him home.

The cell phone had rung. I answered and heard, "Hello, we would like to meet with you about the open position in Hazelden spiritual care department."

I explained my trip, ending our brief conversation with, "I will call on the way home." I ended the call and realized the significance of what had just occurred. A few days after I returned from burying my brother, I made the trip to Center City, Minnesota.

"Are you nervous?" Emy asked.

"No, not at all," I replied.

"Then it's right, Mom."

Tall pines and evergreens greeted me; they formed what I later called God's Cathedral. I drove up Pat Butler Drive, named after the man who provided spirit and action to make the place what it is.

It was not my first time up this lane. We had driven a family member up the lane to receive treatment, and for over thirty-five years, I had referred dozens of alcoholics to the place, encouraging them to walk through the doors of Hazelden. Today's trip, though, was unique.

It had happened because of a chance call, an omen, perhaps a way for me to fulfill a promise I had made to God years ago, to give back the program that God had given me. I was about to discuss a position in which I would walk with the suffering at a place that provided hope, a new life.

I walked through the door with bachelor and master's degrees, although I knew full well that I had received my greatest education in the rooms of my home. When I was hired, I continued a distinct education in the walls of Hazelden. It came from the patients.

What began as a treatment facility for priests now treats patients with dignity and respect. "A miracle a minute" is par for the course, and I experienced it myself on what I call sacred ground. Since 1949, the Hazelden Foundation has operated a facility in Center City, Minnesota, that provides treatment and compassion for alcoholics/addicts and their families. Hazelden is a place that has for over sixty years treated the suffering and taught truth.

At Hazelden, I continued to learned facts, some I had known: in 1956, the American Medical Association declared alcoholism an illness; in 1966, it declared it a disease. The new facts continue: in 2011, a four-year process involving more than eighty experts resulted in a new definition:

"At its core," past president of ASAM Dr. Michael Miller stated, "addiction isn't just a social problem or a moral problem or a criminal problem. It's a brain problem whose behaviors manifest in all these other areas. Many behaviors driven by addiction are real problems and sometimes criminal acts. But the disease is about brains, not drugs. It's about underlying neurology, not outward actions." The conclusion is something everyone in the field of addiction knows: addiction is a chronic disease and must be treated, managed, and monitored over a person's lifetime.

Alcoholism can cause disorder in, or an abnormal condition of, an organ or other part of an organism. As when a substance causes a negative response when introduced into the body of a person allergic to it, so alcohol can cause particular negative reactions in certain people. It causes disorder in such a person's brain, which then sends signals that give rise to obsessive cravings. The alcohol literally alters that person's brain and body biochemically.

Ultimately, addiction is a physical disease of the brain, caused by exposure to drugs. It begins as a quick fix and fixes quick. We like to say, "First you take a drink. Then the drink takes a drink. Then the drink takes you." The power of the disease is that, once started, a person can't stop, using again even when he or she says, and believes, "Never again." The brain is high jacked. Anesthetized. And it's a progressive disease, not a moral issue. It causes destruction to the afflicted person's spirit. There's no instant cure. No easy cure.

The costs to the human family are incalculable. The disease takes everyone in its wake. Alcoholism is cunning, powerful, baffling. It is a disease that takes the sufferer to the edge of insanity, and for some, to total insanity. Others become sober from shear will power. No longer drinking, is called sobriety. Recovery is different. Recovery heals the spirit.

It is a spiritual "dis-ease." Carl Jung, the noted Swiss psychiatrist, stated it well and is often quoted: *spiritus contra spiritum*. It is a Latin phrase that loosely means: alcohol (*spritus*) against (*contra*) the spirit (*spiritum*). In this view, alcoholism is about trying to fill some void with alcohol or spirits when really the search is one of the spirit for something greater than ourselves, for God.

Jung said that the alcoholic's craving for alcohol "was the equivalent, on a low level, of the spiritual thirst of our being for wholeness, expressed in medieval language: the union with God." Later he wrote,

> I am strongly convinced that the evil principle prevailing in this world leads the unrecognized spiritual need into perdition if that is not counteracted either by real religious insight or by the protective wall of human community. An ordinary man [or woman] not protected by an action from above and isolated in society, cannot resist the power of evil, which is called very aptly the Devil.

Carl Jung believed that the only way an alcoholic could recover was through a spiritual experience, a connectedness with a Higher Power. In most traditions, this power is God, but one can understand it simply as a Higher Power of one's own experience or understanding. The only patients, Dr. Jung reflected, he had seen overcome their alcoholism were those who attained the "union with God."

Bill W., Dr. Bob, and the healers at Hazelden all teach that, without living a spiritual program, a program of recovery is difficult. While some people gain sobriety, not all reach recovery, which entails going to a deeper core to fill the void; recovery provides humility through self-understanding and an understanding of others. Without it, even a sober person can become restless, irritable, discontent, and miserable. So do their families. For most, recovery means living the twelve steps of Alcoholics Anonymous, where love is offered not imposed.

When diseases like leprosy or Hanson's disease hit the planet, the suffers were quarantined, hidden away. Damian of Molokai knew it and walked with the lepers. Alcoholism has been treated similarly. Sister Ignatia knew it. So did Bill W. and Dr. Bob. Examples of those who fought for those who suffered. Damian, Bill, and Bob taught the way of loving the sufferer. And they knew the prospects were daunting.

Healing the spirit in recovery is the art of a homecoming based on the quality of our relationship with ourselves, others, and a Higher Power. The values and feelings that the disease suppresses often come back, sometimes with a vengeance, causing tremendous shame and guilt. Addressing these flaws and returning to the basics of a virtuous life is a phenomenon of recovery. This takes courage, as well as a pursuit of justice, service, compassion, self-control, and a profound spirituality.

Through recovery, the separated become reunited. Life begins anew. Truly, recovery is a passage from death to resurrection. It is the fundamental paradox. Scripture, the Torah, the Koran, and other sacred books all call us in the human struggle to recover from separation. That truth surfaces in recovery, in living the twelve steps as way of life.

Damian McElreth, mentor, friend, writer, historian, formidable, and longtime and former Franciscan priest, wrote several books on the history of the place. His most recent, *Essence of Twelve Step Recovery*, captures the miracle and gift of working in an environment based on the twelve steps of AA.

Damian speaks of a person's search for a Higher Power using the metaphor of the sacraments. A Higher Power is the visible sign of an invisible presence. We find sacrament in Nature, literature, music, art, and children. At Hazelden, as when working an AA program, patients find it through "the group" of mutual suffers in the disease. They share their stories and find they are not alone. In the group, relating as one alcoholic to another, they find support, encouragement, the same way Bill W. and Dr. Bob did: by sharing their stories. And they find their core goodness, which they often felt has been lost in the throes of the disease, and they find it by following Hazelden's historical and simple spiritual protocol.

1. Make your bed.
2. Be respectful of one another.
3. Attend lectures on the twelve steps.
4. Talk to one another.

The fascinating history of Hazelden inspires treatment facilities throughout the world. In 1950, Dan Anderson, the staff psychologist at Willmar State Hospital in Willmar, Minnesota, saw the value of Alcoholics Anonymous for the patients who were allowed to attend outside AA meetings. He made the twelve steps of AA the foundation of what later would be called the Minnesota model.

Patrick Butler, a driving force behind the success of Hazelden, brought Anderson and the model to Hazelden, establishing an understanding of alcoholism primarily as a disease of the body, mind, and spirit. The development of a multidisciplinary approach to treatment followed, since the disease is multiphasic and affects people physically, neurologically, mentally, emotionally, and spiritually.

The holistic, multidisciplinary approach involves a team of professionals from all disciplines and includes addiction counselors, spiritual-care counselors, psychologists, psychiatrists, physicians, recreational therapists, dieticians, and as important are those who provide transportation, maintenance, cooking, and cleaning treat the disease. Their work with those suffering with alcoholism happens on sacred ground, where's there's miracle a minute.

~

"There it is," I said quietly. Goosebumps covered my skin. I was making the pilgrimage.

The trip had begun in Stowe, Vermont, at the Trapp Family Lodge. *The Sound of Music* von Trapp family. Like my favorite childhood story, *Heidi*, *The Sound of Music* spoke to me. I was bathed in the innocence of the late 1950s and early 1960s when the movie first came out.

Having settled in the United States after leaving the Nazi regime, the von Trapps lived among the splendor of the magnificent Green Mountains of Vermont, surrounded by a stunning blue haze; the mountains were a reminder of the von Trapp's beloved Swiss Alps. The family built an Austrian-style lodge, with a bakery and fine dining, providing sustainable foods to their visitors.

As a visitor to the lodge, I felt the spirit and tenacity of Maria. Before arriving, I knew the major role that her Catholic faith played in Maria's life but once there, I learned more about her life. I learned of Maria's hard childhood, due to the death of her parents when she was only six years old. Although baptized Catholic as an infant, she was raised by an anti-Catholic guardian who alienated her from her early love of Bible stories and Catholic traditions.

These, however, were restored later in her adulthood, when drawn by the music, she went to Mass at a Jesuit church. Later, this strong-willed, impetuous young woman, with her refound faith, knocked on the doors of Nonnberg

Convent. She entered the noviate of the Benedictine abbey. And what followed is history.

I felt the energy of all the von Trapps, who lived out their lives in their adopted home after World War II. I visited the graves of the Captain von Trapp, Maria, and the deceased von Trapp children, their final resting places beside the lodge. I hiked to the chapel erected by the second-oldest son, Werner. He built the stone chapel in the hills as a monument to Our Lady of Peace, in thanks for having survived World War II. It is a place of exquisite beauty tucked between the mountains, a place of serenity.

My stay there fed my spirit. It is a place connected to all that is Catholic. A place that is imperfectly perfect, just like Maria.

My departing drive from Stowe to East Dorset that fall Vermont morning was beautiful, the mountains and woods splashed with crimson, gold, and burgundy. I couldn't help but reflect on how Vermont and its stoic Vermonters have influenced my life: Bill W., Dr. Bob, Maria Von Trapp, the monks at Weston Priory, and Ben and Jerry.

While my own road to recovery began at Saint Mary's Church, it came full circle thirty-five years later on that Vermont trip. Lost on Highway 7A, looking for the Wilson House, I glanced to my left. A cemetery. As if a force turned the wheel, I drove in; again, I looked to my left. A headstone. "Wilson," it read. Small American flags had been pushed into the dirt. Adorning the grave were holy cards, flowers, notes, and a dish filled with medallions. Next to Bill's headstone was another. Lois. Two lives that caused a sea change.

Overcome, tears flowing without reserve, I realized I had company. A man was sitting, perched, on a riding lawn-mower, with a watchful eye. I walked toward him.

"Are there many people who come here?" I asked.

A smile began to creep up the side of his mouth. "Yes. Forty, fifty..."—and then a pregnant pause—"a day." Continuing, he said, "They come from all over the world."

My voyage to Bill Wilson's birthplace in East Dorset, Vermont, was like my first Al-Anon meeting: coming home. I looked around the cemetery. There they were. The multiple names of the characters who had played a role in their lives. Gillman Wilson. Emily Griffith Wilson. Bill's genetic pool. And Mark Whalon, friend who became the surrogate brother, father figure, uncle, his own Mark Twain. The people who gave him life. Unsuspecting Vermonters used as a vessel to change the world.

The trip to that small piece of land in Vermont answered a question I had asked myself for years: "Why have I always been more drawn to Bill Wilson than to Lois?" Like my attraction to John Fitzgerald Kennedy and his childhood, my draw to Bill W. was based on his emotional character and on the fact that his life and background reflected my own. We lived rather similar lives and sometimes acted in similar ways, except for the drinking. We also were impacted by some of the similar behavior patterns from our respective mothers: Rose Kennedy, Emily Griffin Wilson, and LaVerna Braun Sanow Kittelson.

I wanted to find the lake, the place where he played, fell in love, and as a naïve thirteen-year-old heard his aloof mother, say to him and Dorothy, his only sibling, "Your father and I are divorcing. He is leaving. I am going away to school." She left the two young siblings in the care of their stern but loving grandparents, Fayette and Ella Griffith. Thus began a tailspin that played out over the rest of Bill's life.

Emerald Lake State Park contains a green lake, its name due to marble dust from the quarries nearby. Vermont Marble: the place his people worked. Few white birches are left, but there are beautiful evergreens, and the wind blew through their branches and across my face that warm autumn day. Two mountain ridges framed each side. It was tranquil, serene. I could almost hear Bill and Lois laughing.

Canoe paddles broke the silence as a young couple slowly glided by, adding to the peaceful setting. Standing at the edge of the lake, I dipped my feet into the clear, cool water. Down the beach were sunbathers. In the water, swimmers greeted a perfect day.

Emerald Lake is where he met and fell in love with the young woman from New York, Lois Burnham. They went on to forge a life together. That history began at this beautiful lake. And before that, this lake reflected his childhood joy and grief. This is where Bill learned to swim. It was a place where he played as a young boy, well before he could even imagine the two cups of shared coffee, multiple coffee pots, Dr. Bob, Father Ed Dowling, womanizing, homelessness, Stepping Stones, Wits End, and AA. When he was a boy in this place and in his small village—in that boy's world— he had no idea that he was to influence millions of lives or cause a worldwide phenomenon.

Not long after visiting the lake, I walked across the threshold of Bill Wilson's generational home, what is lovingly called the Wilson House. In the bedroom of that boarding house, which also had a bar to serve drinks, is where William Griffin Wilson, the cofounder of Alcoholics Anonymous, was born. His mother, Emily Griffith Wilson, was also born in this small hamlet. As a mother, she treated her son with the same lack of emotion I received from my mother.

Perhaps it was due to her husband's alcoholism or perhaps it boiled down to the basic personality with which she was born. Either way, she had a choice about how to relate to her son. She had reason. And she must have had a heart.

His father was bore here as well. Gilliman Wilson, gregarious and alcoholic. The Wilsons lived with their two children in the safe, secure, tiny village of East Dorset, Vermont, until the disease changed their lives.

The generational Wilson home functioned as a boarding house, providing respite for travelers from Canada to Albany and as far away as Boston and New York. It was similar to my family's Dakota Hotel; Bill's family was in the hospitality business. Today, the Wilson House provides hope to the recovering soul.

Later that evening, in one of the rooms in which Bill romped as a child, I attended an open AA meeting. A woman with a warm smile greeted me with "Welcome home," and slipped a chip in my hand. After over thirty years in the program, I received my first recovery chip at Bill W.'s house. So very fitting.

People entered the room, and the Wilson House filled with laugher; it literally rolled around the room. My mind flashed back to the cemetery. Lois and Bill. His wife, Lois Burnham Wilson, lay beside Bill W. in the beautiful Vermont landscape, surrounded by those they loved and who loved them. All who frequented this space. And I thought of Bill's childhood friend and drinking buddy, Ebby Thacher, who had been laid to rest in another cemetery.

Ebby had essentially brought the program of recovery to Bill that fateful day in New York. Bill, hungover, had thought his drinking buddy was coming to share another drink, and then perhaps another and another. When the doorbell rang and

Bill opened the door, he found a sober Ebby. Clean, spotless, and sober.

When Bill pushed a drink toward Ebby on the simple table in Bill and Lois's equally simple kitchen, Ebby pushed it back. Something happened. There and then began the story of Alcoholics Anonymous, the legacy of which I was experiencing at the Wilson House seventy-five years later. Because of Ebby's simple act, millions have recovered through the twelve-step program.

The majestic Mt. Aeolus protectively guards the small town in which the cofounder of AA was born. It is the mountain where Bill's grandfather had a spiritual experience, which itself was a portent of what was to happen to his grandson years later.

A few days later, I left East Dorset and drove through the Catskills to Bedford Hills, New York, located in Westchester County. My destination: a small house named "Stepping Stones." It is nestled in a tree-lined neighborhood, tucked between massive, hundred-year-old trees, flourishing bushes, and mounds of flowers. Hollyhocks, Vermont rhubarb, and antique roses frame the home of Bill and Lois, where they lived the last thirty-some years of their life.

Walking across the threshold, I felt as though I were entering the home of a friend or beloved family member. It felt as though the owners were simply on an errand and would return within minutes. It was lovely. I walked the beautiful wooden floors, looking at the mementos, the piano he bought for Lois in their early days of marriage, his violin, the coffee pot, cups, chairs, and table.

I sat down with a man from Switzerland, a woman from Germany, and another from Pennsylvania. My visit to this special place fulfilled all of the seven desires that ever the human being has: to be heard, affirmed, blessed, safe, touched, chosen, and included. I truly felt the reality of the twelve steps of Alcoholic Anonymous, as well as the reality of that which is bigger than any and all of us: whether you call a Higher Power, God, Allah, Great Spirit, Buddha, or the Universe.

The message I felt was this: you are welcome at the table. I had experienced this sense of welcome at Saint Patrick's in Lead, South Dakota, Saint Mary's, and now at the Wilson's home. When I said to myself that first time at Saint Patrick's "I want what they have," I got what I wanted. I had never met the people sitting with me at the table in Bill and Lois's kitchen before that moment, but our different worlds, with our common experiences, had brought us together. And it enabled us to do what Bob and Bill had done. We "passed it on."

Chapter 20

McIntosh. One hundred years old. The four remaining children of Harry and LaVerna returned to celebrate our roots, in the town where everyone knew everything about everyone. The good and the bad. The only paved street in town, except for old Highway 12, was still the only paved road in town. Most of the stores I remembered were now torn down, including the Dakota Hotel, our home. The few remaining buildings were painted and decked out to the hilt for the celebration.

A new clinic and post office stood proudly in two of the former vacant lots. Their presence spoke of progress. We visited the new post office. I looked for box 262, our family box for our entire life in McIntosh. This little town had changed, just as our phone number had changed from 3-4392 to 273-4392 and later to 605-273-4392.

I thought of how many times my fingers had dialed the number and how many times I had looked in the window of box 262 to see if a much-waited letter had arrived. Dad got the mail every morning; however, sometimes all the mail was not sorted and a surprise lurked in the little box later in the day. I especially remember when Patrick Joseph worked on his uncle's farm during the summer. He sent me letters. Enclosed were special items. I sent him a box with mementos.

The anniversary celebration packed the main street, the older generations reminiscing and younger generations making new memories. As we walked the main street of our youth, I reflected on my memories of this street. The times we drove these short blocks with Mom and Dad to church, to school and school activities, with Dad to pick someone up or take someone home.

On this street we marched in the McIntosh High School marching band during the homecoming parades. It was on the street that my friend Paulette and I met to listen to "Bobbie's Girl," drink Pepsi, and eat peanuts at Ma Schneider's Recreation Hall. It was where Vonnie and I ate candy from Ed Robb's candy store and Tony and Leona's grocery store. It was the street where our hotel greeted people from all over the world. It was also the street we drove cars for the first time, legally and sometimes illegally.

It was also the street where Vonnie was struck and later lay dying. Yes, I reflected on this street. This town held many memories. It was home. As my sisters, Mary and Cece, and brother Wally walked, we stopped and reminisced with people. Harry and LaVerna entered every conversation, and many stories were salt and peppered with mention of Joe.

I wrote a poem that reflects my love for this place.

McINTOSH
Green hamlet
Ed Robb's candy counter
Ridge for small toes to peak.
Gravel roads, farmer's loads
Main Street paved.

One mile long.
McIntosh High south end a tall Evergreen
Yielding to lives too quickly pass
City Park—Dr. Pitts dead
Saint Bonaventure's white steeple
Guided, guarded.
The town of childhood
Safe, secure, pure
Marge's ripe, red, succulent tomatoes and more.
—Annetta Sanow Sutton

Yes, home for me included two towns: Montrose, the one of my birth, and McIntosh, the one of my youth. Two completely different communities. One primarily Irish, the other, German. And to this day, upon entering Montrose and McIntosh, the communities that created and formed me, my heart leaps. I am home.

~

"Can I talk to you alone?" Jack asked me, sitting across the table in my sister's house. I was in South Dakota.

Jack, Wally, and I had been sipping coffee. After attempting to have a common discussion, Jack gave up. Wally was in no mood. He was angry. Wally was sitting across the table from the man who had hurt his sister. Although the two had drank together more than once, Wally never saw their similarities.

He never saw the fact his two families had been destroy because of alcoholism and the associated behavior. He never saw the fact that, like Jack, he, too, had destroyed the love his wives felt toward him. He never realized the impact of his drinking on his children and the loneliness of growing old without the joy of knowing his grandchildren. Wally's anger prompted him to leave my sister's house in the middle of the night without saying good bye. I never saw him alive again.

I sat at the table between these two men I loved and who had deeply influenced my life, the one from the moment of my birth and the other from the moment of giving new life to the first of our five children. Both men lost to the throes of a disease from which I could not save them, nor would they let me. As I sat between the two of them, I thought, "This is my life. This has been my life. With one exception. Through understanding the joy of the Easter story of resurrection, by having received the gift of recovery, I am alive. Totally alive."

Chapter 21

The Hebrew word for breath is *ruah*. *Ruah* is spirit. I kept saying to myself "*Ruah. Ruah.*" My children coached me, saying, "Mom, you are the only one who can do this. You are the only one who will honor him." I listened to the voices of my children.

It was another eulogy, although, it wasn't called a eulogy. Wally had died alone at his son's home in Pennsylvania. He had been attending the last basketball game of the season at the university where his son was coach. The death certificate would say that he died of a heart attack, complicated by diabetes. But I knew better.

I had been eliminated from the funeral service. Specifically dismissed. I knew why. I had been told that my only contributions could just be a few funny stories at the planned dinner. I didn't do as I was told. Not this time. Like arranging for the suburban for Dad's funeral, I did what I wanted to. I was not to be dismissed. Not again. No one was going to tell me what I could do and say. Therefore, I gave another eulogy. At the dinner. Why? Because he was my brother.

I stood at the dinner following the funeral and heard myself say, "On behalf of Wally's children and sisters, I welcome you." I continued, "Wally loved toasts. Wally was a gourmet cook. French cooking was his specialty. His appetite began in the little kitchen in South Dakota where Mom baked homemade chocolate cake with homemade chocolate frosting. Wally ate the entire cake. Rail thin his entire life but with a ferrous appetite, he never gained weight."

Nonstop, I continued to tell those present about my brother. "Aspects of my brother, including his talents, were unknown to others. He had been an exquisite pianist, until teased unmercifully by his male peers. Then he stopped. His dancing reminded people of Fred Astaire's. Athletically gifted, he set records that stood for a number of years in our high school. A picture of him and his team commemorates the 1962 state basketball team. Theirs was the first such team from our little school to make state. It was a time in our little town when the world stopped."

My heart beat furiously. I wanted the people sitting in the chairs, including his three children, even his two younger sisters, to really know the man we were burying.

"For me, his sister, he was so much more. Although we moved when Wally was ten years old, his life began in Montrose, the simple, safe Irish hamlet. It was there, just after our dad died, that a well-meaning person told him, 'Wally, you are now the man of the house. Take care of your mother and your sisters.' He did. As a child, my oldest brother was our hero. Our father died when he was eight. I was just pass two. He took his role seriously, protectively watching over his three sisters.

"His role changed again a few years later, when Mom married our second father. Three more children were born to their union. My brother, along with his athleticism, was intellectually gifted. He entered the FBI Academy in Washington, DC. The world, so it seemed, was his oyster. For over a year he immersed himself in the FBI. Then came November 22, 1963, and J. Edgar Hoover. A convergence of events included the assassination of John F. Kennedy. Wally, brought up with a different type of law enforcement, became disillusioned when he knew that so much of the truth was being sanitized.

"Then when two of his sisters died less than two years apart—one was sixteen, the other, twenty-one—he was never the same. This protective brother could not protect his beloved sisters from a drunk driver or ruptured appendix. He numbed his grief with alcohol. A diagnosis of diabetes did not deter him from drinking. Years later, the progression took its toll. The realities of his drinking were significant. The carnage and impact in all aspects of his life were apparent. Lost marriages, children, employment, homes, and yes, even his life."

My mind rushed back to a few months before his death.

"I want to attend Jodie's wedding," I had told him, referring to his daughter's wedding. "Do you think she will invite me?"

"Yes, she will invite you. Do you want to make the trip together?" he had asked.

My brother and I made the trip to Pennsylvania to visit his two oldest children and attend the wedding. We stayed in the same hotel, shared the same room, and drove together in the car we rented. It was sacred time. As we drove, we talked of many things: regrets, losses, the love he still felt for his first love. He made what is called in AA a "fifth step," a kind of confession, to me, his little sister. I encouraged him to make amends to those he had hurt. He did to the mother of his two oldest children and to his children. And his children forgave him. Many times I had been proud to be his sister. This was the proudest moment.

I witnessed God's grace during this trip, and I believe that it is moments like this that show that, through God, all things are possible. It was—is—a reliving of the Easter story. The impact of addiction had separated him from everything he loved. The disease of addiction had taken him away. The unconditional love of God brought him back. I tried many times to help him—it didn't work. He needed something greater than me.

Continuing the dinner speech—I singularly honored each of his children. "You were loved deeply by this imperfect man. Your father wanted to bring his children together in life; instead, he brought you together in death. You come from good people. Tell his grandchildren and their children what a good man he was—imperfect, but good. Tell his story."

I concluded, "Many of you know that my brother and I struggled with one another. I tried to help him. The protector would not be protected. He died too soon. We lost Wally years before. First, his first family lost him, then his second family. Ultimately, he lost his life. A favorite writer, Garrison Keillor, penned on the day of his brother's death—he died on the same day as Wally had—'When your brother dies, you are left disinherited, unarmed, semi-literate, an exile. There is one less person to remember your childhood with.'" I concluded the speech by playing a song he loved. Two of his classmates—best friends, husband and wife—began to dance. Their expression of love and honor was a fitting final tribute to the brother who taught me how our heroes sometimes disappoint us and with the disappointment it reminds us of our own imperfections.

I had felt disinherited prior to Wally's death; however, his death gave me answers to the questions, many questions.

Mom used to say, "You can't go back. . . ." But you have to if certain things were never addressed.

In the midst of the chaos of Wally's death and funeral, I found a box, a dilapidated one—one that supplied answers. A void that had existed from 1952 was about to be filled. I had known my second father better than I had the first. I was about to meet Alfred Johannes Wilhelim Sanow in the dilapidated box.

I returned home from the funeral holding the box, the last vestige of the relationship with my oldest brother. Grief and alcoholism converged. Following Wally's death and the hurt that surrounded it, Wally's belongings were scattered. I found several priceless family mementos in the garbage. These included my mother's First Communion candle from the 1920s. The find, combined with my grief, wracked my body. The box added to it.

Wally had shared many things with me, but he had never shared this: a paint-stained, rusted, beat-up, dilapidated box. The funeral confirmed the feeling that I had felt nearly all of my life, the feeling of being emotionally disinherited. That was about to change.

I stood in my dining room. Outside, the first harbingers of spring were peaking through the brown grass. The difficult winter was melting away. I was emotionally drained. The funeral had been difficult. I stared at the object sitting on my dining room table. My stomach churned.

Hinges creaked as I opened the box that had been made sometime around World War I. Inside the box were some papers and a stack of pictures, grayed, bowed with age. The visages of the people in them were stern. The people were well dressed in clothes from the early 1900s. Prim and proper, some sitting, no smiles, but twinkles in the eyes of the younger ones.

A boy with baby's breath on his lapel stood with a book of scriptures in his hands. Properly combed hair. In another picture were women in long, beautifully designed, home-made dresses. Boys in homemade suits sewn, most likely, by the hands of the mother posing in the picture. On the back of the pictures, various names, none I recognized except the last name. It was the one I was given at birth.

Tucked inside the stack of pictures was a letter, dated 1952, addressed to my mother and her children, which included me. Written in even, beautifully scripted handwriting, it was a letter of condolence at the death of my father. Apologetic. Floods in Kansas. Unable to attend the funeral. The writer offered sympathy. The words flowed off the aged paper. Reading the letter so many years later, I felt my eyes fill with tears. I was moved, yet unaware of the depths of what was to follow. The letter writer, Esther Clare, my father's youngest sister, was long dead.

Something compelled me to go to the computer. I Googled her name. A picture from the dilapidated box jumped up on the screen. It was the front cover of a book titled *My Name is Esther Clare*. My emotions exploded. Tears flowed down my cheeks. My heart pumped as I read the introduction and excerpts from the book. I researched the author and contents. Ecstatic, I mused, "Here, in a book, I may find the answers to my life-long questions, including 'Who really was my father?'"

"Dad." "Father." People take the words for granted. I never have. I spoke these words to him only until I was just passed my second birthday. Heart disease took him. It was the beginning of a void. Emptiness. I never fully understood the impact of his death until I was twenty-seven years old, although I cried as a child quietly at night, missing him. I copied out the song lyrics "How far is heaven, when can I go? To see my daddy, he's there I know. . . ."

Nothing fills the emptiness a child falls into when losing a father through death, divorce, neglect, or worse, apathy. It is profound for a girl. Her ability to fill the void becomes a survival technique. Carl Jung, the noted psychiatrist, said, "There is no birth of consciousness without pain." Dad's death brought me a life of consciousness.

Mom had shared few details of him. Her grief remained raw, making it impossible for her to talk about their lives— our lives—together. The dilapidated box contained further information. A wedding certificate. A love letter. My parents were married in Worthington, Minnesota, in 1939. By a Catholic priest. I was shocked.

I frantically sorted through the box for the answer to a question I had had for so long. The question came from a chance statement made by a relative who had mentioned Dad's first marriage, thinking I knew of it. I hadn't. The relative shared with me that his first marriage had disintegrated due to the death of their only child. The boy had been eight years old. When I asked mother about it, she changed the subject, never to be broached again.

The fact that my parents were married by a Catholic priest means one of a few things about my father's first marriage: that it had been annulled in the Catholic church; that his first wife was not baptized; or that a pastoral priest took them through what is called the internal form. This is where the priest works with a couple, after external means are exhausted, to pastorally conclude, in good conscience, that the marriage had not been a sacramental bond after all. I do not know the answer. But I now know a priest married them.

I have another question that has never been answered. Dad had been raised in a strict Lutheran family; in his family, embracing Catholicism was not an option. And for my very Catholic mother, leaving the church wasn't, either. Did he join the Catholic church? I do know Dad was buried from Saint Patrick's Catholic Church. My very German, Lutheran father ultimately lay among the Irish Catholics in Saint Patrick's Cemetery in Montrose. Ecumenism at its best.

The box contained more startling information. Dad, a World War I veteran, had been twenty-five years older than my mother. I saw from his military discharge card, which almost literally jumped out from the box, that he had served a year and then received an honorable discharge. It had been such a short length of service. Why? The card provided the answer: "Discharged due to having contracted the Spanish Flu."

It had been a historical pandemic, this flu that killed close to fifty million people, about 3 percent of the world's population at the time. It killed between fifty and one hundred million worldwide. Five hundred million infected. Most victims were healthy young adults, in contrast to most influenza outbreaks, that typically affect the very young, the elderly, or weakened patients.

My dad survived the Spanish flu. Reading his service papers, I wondered if the flu caused my father to die prematurely of a heart condition. At the time of his death, he had been thin; he had always been a health nut and was in good shape. Perhaps some remnants of the flu affected his heart. I will never know.

The love letter provided a glimpse into my father's heart

and his love for my mother. He was, it seems, madly in love with her. And she with him. I knew it. The letter was verification.

The book arrived. My father's childhood flowed through the voice of Esther Clare in words penned by her granddaughter, Laurel, a brilliant, published writer. As I began to read, answers to questions that had never been answered, including those I had been afraid to ask, rolled out before my eyes. As a child, I had been told that Dad had hated alcohol. Had he, really? The answer arrived not in the box, but in the book.

It was Emelie who had posed in those pictures that I discovered in the dilapidated box; she was the maker of the homemade dresses and suits worn by her children. She had formed the ten children, with August, in the strictness of their Lutheran faith. It was Dad in the picture with the baby's breath and scriptures. It had been his confirmation. "Alfred Johannes Wilhelim Sanow" read the certificate scripted in German. The pictures spoke of family. They also spoke of solemnity. In the book, the answer came. Grandpa was a stern, authoritarian disciplinarian who kept his children under his controlling protection. As time went on, Grandpa's strict discipline became harsh, abusive, and filled with rage. Grandma had been a recipient of that rage, just as I had suffered at the hands of my husband.

After the ten children were grown and gone, Emelie Sanow did something unheard of in 1924. She, like me, her granddaughter decades later, said, "Enough." She divorced him. My grandfather one of the most successful farmers in Iowa, a solid husband and family man, a faithful Lutheran struck down by a disease. Grandpa was an alcoholic. And Emelie left him. And because of the disease, he lost everything. Everything, including the beautiful rich land that had produced so much. All was lost.

Grandpa died a broken man in 1927.

Grandma lived among her flowers, including her well-cared-for African violets, in a spotless house in Ward, South Dakota, dying in 1955. Prior to her death, she asked to be buried beside Grandpa. I visited their graves. The disease of alcoholism destroyed the tangibles, but the intangibles remained. She loved him; he loved her. In life and in death, their spirits remained together.

My answers came in a dilapidated box, a book, and then in the precious roots of an African violet. The answers had revealed a farm in Iowa and a cemetery close by. Faith and a disease had affected my life long before my birth. My father's, too.

Hiding in a small burgundy ceramic container, an African violet peaked out of the rich soil. Along with it came the instructions:

> *Don't over water your baby violet. They can stand to be dry but not too wet. Grandma Esther always waited until the leaves drooped a little before watering, but I would not wait that long for the baby. I water it a few dribbles of water once a week when the soil feels dry.*
>
> *If you can find a pot a smidge bigger than the one it's in, it probably needs transplanting in a month or so. Don't put it in a big pot. Use a good loamy potting soil*

mix. Violets do better when their roots are pot bound. In the wild they grow in the crooks of trees in tiny amounts of dirt and debris. The more pot bound they are, the better they bloom as they mature. Mine sit in an east window, but they also thrive in a north window. Just imagine. That violet is a start from Emelie's plant, just as we are starts from Grandpa August and Grandma Emelie. That boggles my mind.

Love u, Laurel.

Two granddaughters found one another and a daughter found answers, all because of a dilapidated box, a book, and the deep roots of this African violet.

I wanted to visit the spot where he was born in Cherokee County, Iowa. I returned to the lush Iowa farmland. I held the young violet close. The African violet was first propagated here by the woman who birthed eleven children, one dying and one a stillborn. One hundred and fourteen years ago, on June 10, 1896, the first cries of Alfred Johanne Wilheliem Sanow, my father, were heard on this same land. He had been held in the arms of his gentle mother, fed by the hands that had planted the African violet.

Emelie Schultz Sanow survived the 1871 Chicago fire, homesteaded with August, the only man she ever loved. My father was the youngest male of Emelie's flock. The last born from Emelie's womb was a girl, Esther Clare.

As I stood on the small hill surrounded by the verdant scene, I reflected on the woman who had planted the garden, canned the foods, baked the bread, and bore the children of the man she loved and married walking beside him, feeding, tending, instructing their large flock, supplying the same to the poor of the countryside and the stranger who passed by.

August had come from Prussia, she, from Germany. The seedling of the violet, like my father, began on this soil, toiled by August and Emelie Sanow, my grandparents.

I stood engrossed looking at the hill, imagining Grandma and Grandpa Sanow as they returned from gathering supplies in nearby Marcus, a small town due north. Theirs had been one of the most successful farms in the area. The Sanows had been considered well off.

Still a working farm today, the home the Sanows built is standing and inhabited by another family. Their hen house still functions; the hog barn and smoke house have long since been quiet, but are still standing. The remnants of their barn remain functional with an addition. Over a decade later, the farmstead is still operational; it is evidence of the hard work, perseverance, faith, intelligence, humor, and love born on this fertile Iowa farm. It is testimony to the strength of my grandparents' forged partnership.

As the warm summer wind brushed my face, I felt my father's spirit. I imagined him, his sister Esther Clare and brother August, and the three youngest romping mischievously on the lush green hills, their backdrop cornfields. My body, mind, and spirit filled with long-buried emotions.

As I stood on the rich Sanow soil with the tiny African violet, I was told the story of where the roots began. My cousin, Laurel, was passed the story from her grandmother, Esther Clare. Grandma Emelie had snipped a stem from her own mature plant she received from her mother, my great grandmother, and placed it in fertile soil for her youngest daughter, Esther Clare, who was about to elope and marry the love of her life, Herb Ford.

When Esther and Herb fell in love, Grandma blessed the relationship. Grandpa did not. Grandpa felt Herb was not good enough for his little Esther. He had enumerated certain qualifications that any future husband had to meet. The most important was this: you must marry a Lutheran. Herb was a lapsed Methodist. So Herb and Esther eloped.

Over seventy-five years ago, the cutting from a tiny plant was presented to Esther from her tenacious mother, and this small act of rebellion was not the last time Emelie stood up to August.

The plant, like Esther and Herb Ford's marriage, lasted. A cutting of Esther's violet was presented to me by Aunt Esther's granddaughter, Laurel. Esther Clare brought us together. And it all started with the dilapidated box.

Chapter 22

It was dark, chilly. The lights of the basilica's dome shadowed the figure standing to the side. He had told me to meet him on the side. He said he would watch for me. There in the shadows, he stood. My heart was pumping. Tears filling my eyes, and it felt as if my tear ducts were exploding.

I handed him the bags. "Thanks, Mom," he said.

The bags were brimming with food, socks, sweatshirts, and a blanket. "Where are you staying?" I asked.

"Mom, don't worry. I have it taken care of." And with that, my son walked back into the dark. I sat alone, and the same deep cry that occurred the night of his emergency birth came from deep within. The same disease that took his father away from us was now taking my oldest son.

Thirty-six years after my first Al-Anon meeting, I made the gratitude call. He answered the phone, the mature voice cracking. It was a voice of wisdom.

"Is Ruth available?" I asked. Thirty-six years is a long time. Was she alive? Dead?

Then a faint voice said, "Hello?"

"Ruth, it is Annetta, "I said, my voice choking. I began to cry. "Ruth, I wanted to thank you for saving my life."

She responded with her own tears. "I always wondered what happened to you," she said.

I told her about my life, my recovery, and how her words and encouragement saved my family. In her kitchen, over two cups of coffee, Ruth K. handed me the program that someone had handed her. And with me and countless others, the gift continues.

Standing in Washington State overlooking the breathtaking serenity and beauty of Puget Sound, the summer of 2009, I heard the familiar laughter of my Saint Martin's friends. We had been thirteen years old when we met. The year was 1963. Then, there were seven of us. Six remained. Our coming together was a reflection of the effect that a group of Benedictine nuns had made on us as girls, now women, well-educated women of various professions, mothers, spouses, friends. Women of integrity.

The reunion was a fulfillment of the promise we had made the end of our junior year of high school, a promise to meet every two years. We kept the promise for over forty years. Our friendship remained special, unique. We know it. And it has never waivered through the years. Our friendship began long ago, when we nestled together in the exquisite beauty of the Black Hills with a group of amazing women teaching us to live a good life. They taught. We listened.

The family disease of alcoholism affects every member, whether each one drinks or not. Within the family system, there usually is a designated alcoholic. Although most of the time the rest of the family consumes, too, one person is typically singled out. Jack became the designated alcoholic in our family, and it was followed up by that identification with judgment and criticism.

My brothers' drinking and behavior, especially Wally's, was similar to Jack's. Wally, too, had multiple families that he had abused, emotionally and physically, when intoxicated. His families were marked by financial, medical, and legal irresponsibility. Yet the denial of what was really going on continued, even when the affects of alcoholism were obvious. Wally's diabetes was complicated by drinking, and his drinking was complicated by diabetes. Two diseases. Neither in remission. Both affecting the brain and the ability to make good decisions. One thing is certain: our family has an allergic reaction to alcohol.

"Can I talk to you alone?" Jack had asked me that day sometime before Wally died. The three of us were sitting at my sister's table, drinking coffee. Wally had refused to join in the conversations that Jack had attempted to start.

"Yes," I replied as Wally got up and left us. Once we were alone, Jack looked at me. "I have never stopped loving you," he said.

My response was as honest as his confession has been. "It has never been about not loving each other, Jack. That was always there." I continued, "The disease took so much."

He reached in his back pocket with his good hand; Jack was partially paralyzed from a stroke he had had during an alcohol binge. He opened his billfold. In it was a picture of the children and me; I posed front and center. Jack wasn't in the picture.

I smiled. Jack didn't know the reason for my smile. The photograph was a family picture that we had taken after going to the sacrament of reconciliation, to confession. The children were young. So was I. As with so many events he missed, Jack did not know that, after taking the picture, we lost the state of grace that we had received during the sacrament, due to the kids almost killing each other during the photo shot. It reminded me of the picture of Grandma Emelia and her ten children. Grandpa, too, was not in the picture.

Jack's voice interrupted my reflection. "There is never a day I do not think of you and the kids."

I softly responded, "I know."

"Annetta..." he continued. I thought that funny. During our dating years and the ten years of marriage, even during the worst of the beatings and the horror of the disease, he never called me by my first name. He always called me "dear." When he was intoxicated, he usually followed up "dear" with derogatory word.

"Annetta, I know I hurt you, but I don't remember." I knew he was being honest. In his right mind, this man would not harm a soul. "I used to come to Bismarck, sit across from your home, watch the kids play in the yard." My heart ached for this suffering soul. I knew how he loved his kids. The agony of not being able to play with them must have been painful. He continued, "I did not come to the yard or the door because I was drinking."

I looked at the man with whom I formed five human lives. Together. Alongside a disease and its horror. Alongside recovery and its gifts. The visit was for Jack's sixtieth birthday celebration. I was there to attend.

The party was big, held in the community center, planned by a niece, attended by possibly the entire community. The administrator of the assisted living facility where Jack was living introduced himself to me. He told me how beloved Jack was at the home. I said, "I know. He is a good man." Jack's second wife attended. We visited. Pictures were taken.

No one except God and me knew the extent of my journey with Jack. The gift of reconciliation. Healing from within so I could reconcile, could truly forgive. My faith and the twelve-step program teach reconciliation. In the faith, the journey toward reconciliation begins with baptism. In the twelve-step program, it begins with step one and continues through to step twelve. It is living the paradox of the cross.

We had lived our Good Friday. That celebration with Jack was Easter Sunday. The cross. The 't.' We had come full circle. Good Friday is the pain. Recovery the resurrection.

Forgiveness is not always easy, but it is always necessary. My faith taught me this. So did the twelve steps of AA.

"Mom, I am on the way to the hospital."

Hearing those words, I jumped into my car, the T-shirt printed and ready. I headed to Minneapolis. My heart was in my throat. My first grandchild was on its way.

The baby was born. A boy. I wept. The T-shirt I had brought said, "Born Democrat just like my Grandma." Cameron. My first grandson.

Reed William, Elissa Marie, Maia Elizabeth, Gemma Josephine, Charles Richard, Samuel Joseph, and Isabella Anne followed, each in his or her own turn.

I listen to them chatter. Reed, now at eight years old, said, after finding out that hamburger comes from a cow, "I am going to have to rethink what I am eating."

I drive Elissa and Maia to the Children's Theatre. We're going to see *Annie*. We attend Grandparents Camp. We eat Sonny's Ice Cream. We watch *Toy Story* at the drive-in movie in Cottage Grove. I ask often, "How much does your grandma love you?" In unison comes reply, "High as the moon—and back!"

Their parents sat in similar seats not too long ago. We prayed for the gas fumes to keep the car running. Yes, these new little chirpers came from millionaires. A faith and a program provided the funds.

"Why do you stay?" Catholics are often asked these days. Parishes are closing. Priests have been charged, officially and less officially, with misconduct. Today, there is less a crisis of faith and more a crisis of confidence in the organization. Many of the faithful are disappointed in those we call our leaders. But healing comes from within. It has not happened yet.

The Roman Catholic theological tradition takes the human intellect seriously. We believe that God gave us an intellect and heart. With both, we are to provide for the common good. "Why do we need religion?" some ask. Auschwitz vividly taught us that our lives must have meaning. Victor Frankel calls it Logotherapy. I call it love.

Father Mychal Judge, the priest of compassion who died

in 9/11, showed that love, as did Cardinal Joseph Bernadine, Mother Teresa, and Father Maximillian Kolbe, the priest who asked to be taken to the Auchwitz gas chambers instead of a father of nine. A stranger to Maximillian, but neither were strangers to God. And we find it in the compassionate Father Ed Dowling, as well as gentle lover of alcoholics, Sister Ignatia. We do know to believe is to be committed.

Jesus walks with the suffering in their suffering, and the suffering at this time in the history of the Catholic church is a palpable part of the community. But we also find it in the suffering servant of Christ on the cross and the community of believers. Religion provides structure. Faith teaches us to pay attention. We are to work toward reconciliation. Toward transformation. Toward empathy. Toward love.

The parish I attend encompasses fifty-eight zip codes. People come from all over the cities to a small parish church to be fed from the Eucharist, at the altar, in the pew. And in their lived experience. We find faith in a world of chaos.

And we find it in the next generation. As the procession for Mass begins and the altar servers, followed by the priest, enter the church, my grandson Cameron carries the processional cross. Behind him is his sister and my granddaughter, Elissa Marie. She, too, will serve at the altar. She—the first woman of our family to serve at the altar.

Unknown to Anthony that George Bernard Shaw's quote had long ago become my mantra, he handed me a plaque shortly before his death with that wonderful quotation: "Some people look at things and say why? I dream of things that never were and say why not?" Anthony had the uncanny ability to say just what he wanted with his deep brown eyes. This time he hesitated, drew a breath, and said, "This is you. You just never give up."

My eyes filled. I said, "I can't. I haven't. I won't."

I stand in front of an auditorium filled with recovering alcoholics and their families. My eyes begin to fill. My heart bursts with love and respect. I look the people sitting in front of me in their eyes, for they understand the implausible journey in a way others do not. They know.

And I begin.

Hi, my name is Annetta. I am a grateful, recovering family member.

In gratitude, the cross comes alive.

Epilogue

In writing this book, I experienced a myriad of emotions and memories. It is an intimate story of personal struggle, of redemption. I want to destigmatize alcoholism and Catholicism. Russian writer Dostoyevsky said that many people live their lives without ever finding themselves in themselves. I found myself in both.

Grief begins at birth. And yes, Anthony once told me that everyone is responsible, but no one is to blame. Life is a prolonged farewell. It is a continuous saying good-bye and completion of cycles of growth. I am ready.

Robert Frost wrote about the dawning of a poem, "It begins as a lump in the throat . . . a homesickness, a lovesickness."

Writing this book began the way of homesickness, a lovesickness—with a thought in my head, turned to a knot in my stomach, stuck in my throat, and exploded in my heart. It was like birthing a baby, a true labor of love. If I offended anyone, I apologize. It was not my intent. If I buoyed someone, it is my joy. To those who serve life with me, thank you.

Now I understand what Mom and Dad told us kids on Memorial Day. They said, "Tell the stories."

Mom and Dad, I have.

To LaVerna, Al, and Harry, I owe my life. The quilt of your lives lays over my children, grandchildren, and me in our DNA, features, and faith. To Lois and Bill Wilson, I owe my recovery. To my siblings, I owe understanding, triumph, and tragedies. To Amy, Emy, Jenny, Chet, and Bret, I owe my heart, my life, my love. And to my son-in-laws, Scott, Denny, and Jon, as well as my daughter-in-law, Nicole, I owe my gratitude. To my grandchildren, Cameron, Elissa, Reed, Maia, Gemma, Samuel, Charles, and Isabella, I owe you my spirit. Samantha, thank you for being my first teacher.

Above Grandma Emelie's bed was an embroidered picture with writing in German and made by her mother, who had presented it to Emelie when she married August. After Grandma Emelie died, it was given to her youngest daughter, Esther Clare.

Wo glaube da liebe,
Wo liebe da friede,
Wo friede da segen
Wo segen da Gott
Wo Gott da kine nott.

Roughly translated, it reads;

Where there's hope, there's love,
Where there's love, there is faith,
Where there's faith, there's blessing,
Where there's blessing, there's God,
Where there's God, there is no need.

Resources

1. Sanow Sutton, Annetta. *Our Home on the Prairie*. Self-published, 2007.

2. *Alcoholics Anonymous*. 4th edition. New York: Alcoholics Anonymous World Services, Inc., 2001.

3. Bernardin, Joseph Cardinal. *The Gift of Peace*. Chicago: Loyola Press, 1997.

4. Norris, Kathleen. *Dakota: A Spiritual Geography*. New York: Houghton Mifflin, 1993.

5. McElrath, Damian. *Hazelden: A Spiritual Odyssey*. Center City, MN: Hazelden, 1987.

6. McElrath, Damian. *Patrick Butler: A Biography*. Center City, MN: Hazelden, 1999.

7. McElrath, Damian. *Dan Anderson: A Biography*. Center City, MN: Hazelden, 1999.

8. McElrath, Damian. *Essence of Twelve Step Recovery*. Center City, MN: Hazelden, 2008.

9. O'Donohue, John. *Anam Cara*. New York: Harper Collins, 1997.

10. Johnson, Laurel Smith. *My Name is Esther Clare*. Tempe, AZ: Dandelion Books Publication, 2005.

11. Cheever, Susan. *My Name is Bill*. New York: Washington Square Press, 2004.

12. Borchert, William G.. *When Love is Not Enough*. Center City, MN: Hazelden, 2005.

13. Anderson, William. *The World of the Trapp Family*. Davison, MI: Anderson Publication, 1998.

14. Fitzgerald, Robert S. J. *The Soul of Sponsorship*. Center City, MN: Hazelden, 1995.

15. Royle, Edwin Milton. "De Sunflower Ain't de Daisy."

16. American Society of Addiction Medicine, 4601 North Parke Avenue, Upper Arcade, Suite 101 Chevy Chase, MD 20815-4520

Permission from Weston Priory for "Wherever You Go," 1972, the Benedictine Foundation of the State of Vermont, Inc.